Y0-AUJ-940

DISCARDED

AFTERMATH OF WAR

Bainbridge Colby and
Wilsonian Diplomacy
1920-1921

DANIEL M. SMITH

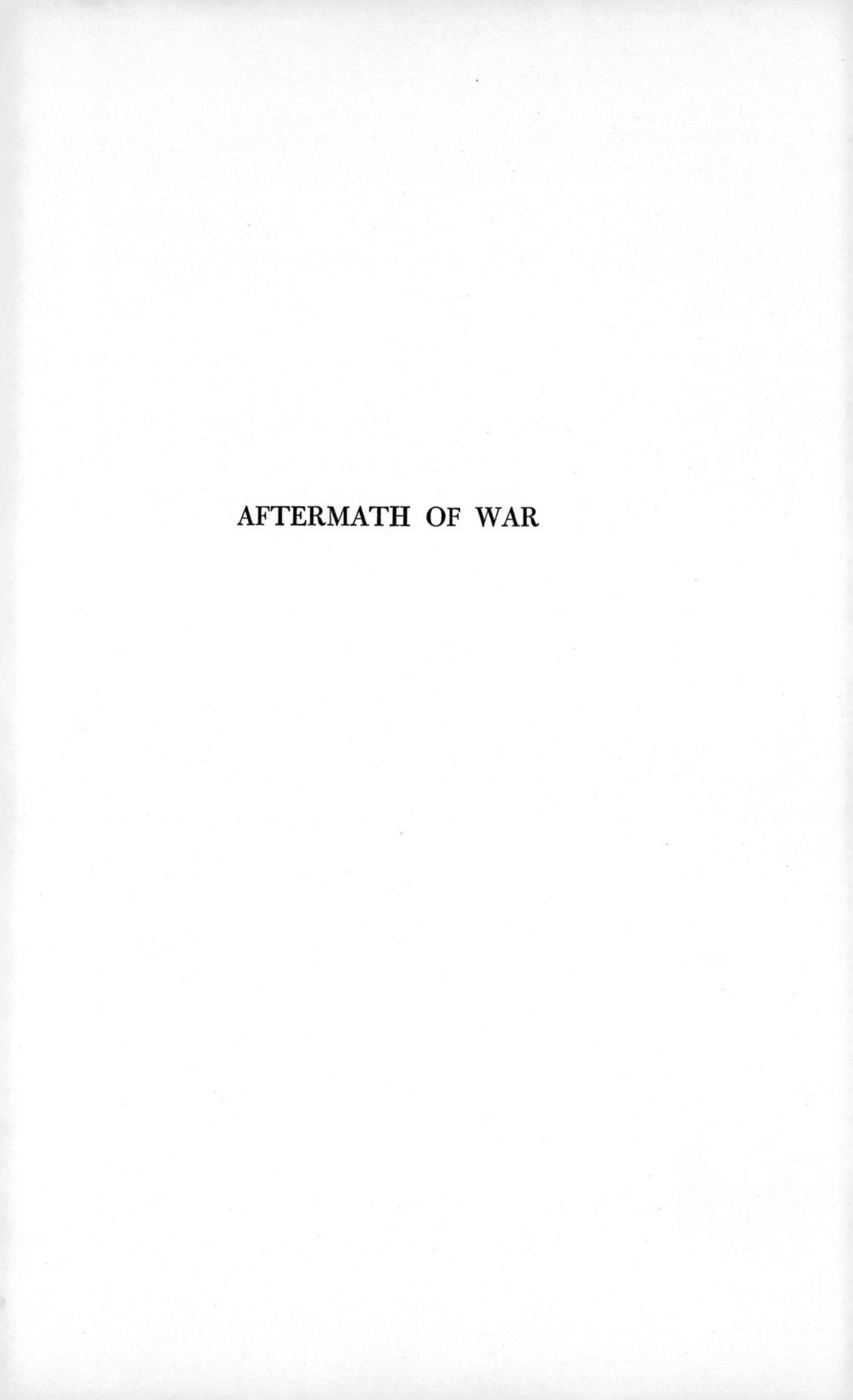

AFTERMATH OF WAR

MEMOIRS OF THE
AMERICAN PHILOSOPHICAL SOCIETY
Held at Philadelphia
for Promoting Useful Knowledge

Volume 80

AFTERMATH OF WAR

Bainbridge Colby
and
Wilsonian Diplomacy
1920-1921

DANIEL M. SMITH
*Professor of History,
University of Colorado*

AMERICAN PHILOSOPHICAL SOCIETY
INDEPENDENCE SQUARE • PHILADELPHIA
1970

Copyright © 1970 by The American Philosophical Society

*Library of Congress Catalog
Card Number 77-115881*

To My Wife, Aladeen

The author acknowledges with gratitude the support of grants from the American Philosophical Society and the Council on Research and Creative Work of the Graduate School of the University of Colorado. Mr. John Crossette has been of invaluable assistance in research.

Contents

	PAGE
Introduction	1
I. A Progressive as Secretary of State	7
II. Europe: Discord with the Allies	32
III. East Asia: Anglo-American Cooperation	75
IV. A New Era in Relations with Mexico	102
V. Retreat from Interventionism	117
IV. Wilson's Secretaries of State	155
Bibliography	160
Index	167

AFTERMATH OF WAR

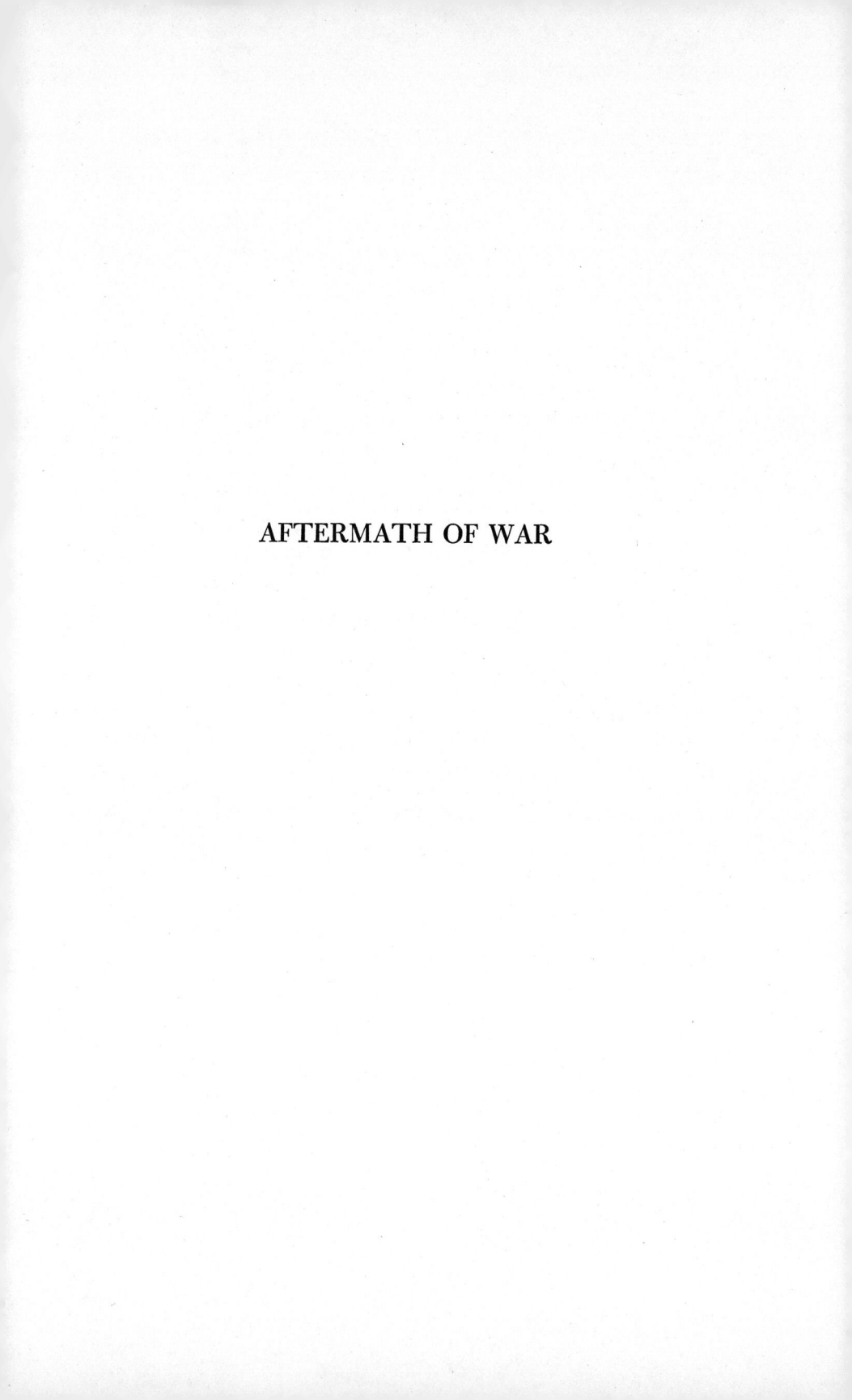

Let us close our ears to the siren voices of the reservationists and the constitutional amenders, and let it no more be said that the United States, in company with revolutionary Mexico, unspeakable Turkey, and Bolshevist Russia, prefers to block and thwart rather than to promote this great step [League of Nations] toward a better world and a nobler life.

—Bainbridge Colby, June, 1920

Introduction

ALTHOUGH there have been numerous published studies on the personalities and events of the Wilson administration, little attention has been given to the career and contributions of Bainbridge Colby, President Woodrow Wilson's third and last Secretary of State. His predecessors in that position, William Jennings Bryan (1913-1915) and Robert Lansing (1915-1920), undoubtedly have merited the many accounts that bear in whole or part upon their careers. Momentous events in East Asia, Latin America, and Europe, and above all the outbreak of the First World War, presented Bryan and Lansing with repeated opportunities to make their impress upon the diplomacy of the times. Colby has been virtually ignored, his tenure in the State Department apparently too short and too late in the Wilson era to be viewed as anything but anticlimactic.[1]

Closer scrutiny, however, reveals that Colby was able to make a significant impress upon at least one area of American foreign relations: Latin America. Even in other areas, involving problems concerned with terminating World War I, strengthening the Open Door in East Asia, and persuading Japan to adopt a more cooperative course, Colby while unable to resolve these problems because of his brief tenure and the unpromising domestic political situation at least grappled with them and pointed the way to their ultimate settlement in the Twenties. Far more than historians have recognized, the Wilson-Colby foreign policy indicated the

[1] A recent work on American Secretaries of State in this century, *An Uncertain Tradition* (New York, 1961), edited by Norman Graebner, omits Colby from the list.

1

approach that the succeeding Republican administrations were to follow, the middle-road path of limited internationalism without assumption of binding political or military obligations abroad. Of course, the Wilson-Colby "neo-isolationism" was more or less forced upon them by the defeat of the Versailles Treaty in the Senate, but it also seems to have reflected President Wilson's personal embitteredness and a growing suspicion of the motives of the major Allied Powers. Colby remained a committed Wilsonian internationalist, to the last hopeful of entering the League of Nations. He subscribed fully to the vision of a "peaceful liberal capitalist world order," within which the American industrial giant would be preeminent and prosperous.[2]

It has been pointed out that an American President has tended to select his first Secretary of State primarily upon political considerations, but that if the opportunity arose he felt freer to make second and third choices for that position on other grounds.[3] The choice of Colby early in 1920, following Bryan and Lansing, illustrates that point.

It was obvious to his contemporaries that politics explained Bryan's appointment to head the State Department in 1913. The Democratic presidential nominee in 1896, 1900, and 1908, Bryan had millions of loyal admirers and supporters from the days of his crusades against Wall Street and the trusts. Moreover, he could contribute to the domestic legislative program of the new Wilson administration. Thus although he had written, in 1904, that Bryan "has no brains,"[4] the President-elect had felt it necessary to appoint the Great Commoner to the premier Cabinet

[2] For a stimulating reinterpretation of Wilsonian liberal internationalism, see N. Gordon Levin, Jr., *Woodrow Wilson and World Politics: America's Response to War and Revolution* (New York, 1968).

[3] Alexander de Conde, *The American Secretary of State, An Interpretation* (New York, 1962), pp. 44-46.

[4] As quoted in Harley Notter, *The Origins of the Foreign Policy of Woodrow Wilson* (Baltimore, 1937), p. 65.

post. Despite so inauspicious a beginning, relations between President Wilson and Secretary Bryan at first seemed most satisfactory. Not that Wilson ever revised his intellectual estimate of Bryan—he once said that he would run again for the presidency if necessary to forestall Bryan, whose elevation to the White House in Wilson's view would be both a personal and a national disaster.[5] Bryan was useful domestically, however, and seemed cooperative and fully conscious of his secondary role in foreign affairs to the President and to his intimate private adviser, Colonel Edward M. House. As the Colonel recorded early in 1913, Wilson reported that Bryan "was a constant surprise . . . amenable to advice, did not talk unduly much and was altogether different from what he had anticipated." [6]

Yet eventually President Wilson came to regard Bryan as an encumbrance and to anticipate his departure from the Cabinet. In part, it was a reaction to a series of petty irritants: Bryan's sloppy and almost illegible handwritten letters and notes, his clumsy relations with the press, and, more seriously, his inefficient administration of the State Department. Moreover, Bryan unquestionably was poorly suited by experience and ability for his high position. Wilson might ignore the widespread public criticism and amusement caused by Bryan's homey habits and tastes—in addition to his substitution of grape juice for alcoholic beverages at official functions and his Chautauqua lecturing for pay, Bryan personally shopped for groceries, sometimes carried a workman's luncheon pail to the State Department, and was an inelegant dresser—but he could not remain unaffected by Bryan's divergent views on neutrality policies toward the European belligerents and especially his objections to the President's strict accountability stand toward Germany's submarine warfare. On one occasion, late in

[5] Arthur Walworth, *Woodrow Wilson* (2 v., New York, 1958) **2:** f.n., p. 6.
[6] April 1, 1913, House Diary, The Papers of Edward M. House (Yale University Library).

1914, the President remarked to House that because of the World War his administration would be judged by posterity primarily on its foreign policy. Wilson, according to the Colonel, then spoke "with extreme regret of Mr. Bryan's unsuitability for the office of Secretary of State," and intimated that if Bryan ever revealed an inclination to resign over an issue of policy it would be in the best interests of the administration and the country to let him go.[7] Clearly he thought that Bryan had outlived his usefulness, and though he expressed genuine emotion when the Secretary did resign over the U-boat issue in early June, 1915, the President must have felt a sense of relief.[8]

Robert Lansing, Bryan's successor in the State Department, obviously was a non-political appointee. Never prominently identified with national politics, although he was a Democrat, and without a personal political following, Lansing's assets were his great knowledge and experience with international law and diplomacy. The son-in-law of former Secretary of State John W. Foster, Lansing had shared in Foster's international legal practice and had served as counsel for the United States government at a number of arbitrations. In 1914 he had been appointed Counselor or second-in-command of the State Department. In that position Lansing had helped to compensate for Bryan's diplomatic inexperience and poor administration, and he had had a major role in shaping neutrality policies during the European War in 1914-1915. Disciplined, discreet, and reserved, Lansing seemed to President Wilson in mid-1915 to be the ideal replacement for Bryan. He was experienced and there seemed to be every assurance that he would willingly follow the President's lead in foreign affairs, putting notes in the proper diplomatic form and advising when asked upon the intricacies and forms of international diplomacy. When

[7] December 3, 1914, *ibid.*
[8] June 24, 1915, *ibid.* See Arthur S. Link, *Wilson: The Struggle for Neutrality, 1914-1915* (Princeton, 1960), pp. 364-425.

Lansing expressed some doubts about his political qualifications for the office, at a White House interview on June 23, 1915, Wilson brushed that aside with the assertion that foreign policy took precedence over politics at that point of time, and that he and Lansing fortunately were "of the same mind concerning international policies." [9]

Initially, the President was greatly pleased with his new Secretary of State.[10] Lansing got along well with the press and the diplomatic corps, ran a smoother and happier department, and deferred to the President and his adviser, Colonel House. Eventually, however, disillusionment again set in at the White House. Lansing proved to be more realistic and conservative in diplomacy than Wilson and House, and was critical of their mediation efforts and their plans for a liberal postwar order capped by a League of Nations. Contrary to Wilson's assumption in 1915, Lansing's mind often did not follow his chief's and he was unwilling to remain a mere clerk or to subordinate uncritically his judgment to that of the President. His divergence with Wilson's views and policies became more pronounced after the United States entered the war against Germany in April of 1917, and became irreconcilable during the Paris Peace Conference in 1919. Long before then Wilson was anxious to rid himself of a subordinate that he regarded as inadequate and increasingly as disloyal. In early 1916 the President made it clear that he would conduct foreign relations as he deemed best, regardless of Lansing's sensitivities, while Mrs. Wilson complained of the Secretary's "bad judgment." [11] A year later, Wilson described Lansing as the most unsatisfactory member of his Cabinet, fit only for second place because "he had no imagination, no constructive ability, and but little real ability of any

---

[9] June 23, 1915, Lansing Desk Diary, The Papers of Robert Lansing (Library of Congress, Manuscripts Division).
[10] August 26, 1915, House Diary; and August 30, 1915, Lansing Desk Diary.
[11] March 28, 30, 1916, House Diary.

kind." [12] He seriously considered dismissing Lansing on several occasions, in late 1916 when the Secretary objected to mediation efforts, in the summer of 1917 as problems of mobilization increased, and again at Paris during the peace negotiations when Lansing made clear his opposition to League plans and sulked at repeated presidential snubs and by-passing. Wilson was dissuaded each time, however, by the exigency of events or by the intercessions of Colonel House, who preferred the existing relationship where Lansing presumably dealt with routine while House functioned as unofficial foreign secretary. After Wilson began to recover from the stroke or cerebral thrombosis that he suffered in early October of 1919, he was no longer willing to endure what he regarded as disloyalty. Ostensibly because Lansing had called unauthorized meetings of the Cabinet during his illness, but actually for larger reasons, he dismissed the Secretary in early February, 1920.[13]

Lansing's resignation cleared the way for Wilson's last and most satisfactory appointment of a Secretary of State. Bainbridge Colby, as the following account undertakes to show, not only established a far more workable relationship between the State Department and the Chief Executive, but despite the brevity of his tenure in office he also was able to make a sizable impress upon foreign relations during the close of the Wilson administration.

[12] March 28, 1917, *ibid.*
[13] For a fuller account of the Lansing-Wilson relationship and the resignation, see Daniel M. Smith's *Robert Lansing and American Neutrality, 1914-1917* (Berkeley, 1958); and "Robert Lansing and the Wilson Interregnum, 1919-1920," *The Historian* **21** (1959): pp. 135-161.

I. A Progressive As Secretary of State

Let us close our ears to the siren voices of the reservationists and the constitutional amenders, and let it no more be said that the United States, in company with revolutionary Mexico, unspeakable Turkey, and Bolshevist Russia, prefers to block and thwart rather than to promote this great step [League of Nations] toward a better world and a nobler life.
—Bainbridge Colby, June, 1920

As THE EDITORS of *Current Review* commented (in reference to Lansing's volume on *The Peace Negotiations*), "In the two most critical periods of his administration, President Wilson has been unfortunate in having for Secretary of State a man whose mind was hopelessly at variance with his own." [1] That deficiency was finally corrected in the last year of Wilson's administration, when he appointed Bainbridge Colby as his third Secretary of State.

1.

Bainbridge Colby, like Wilson's first Secretary of State, Bryan, was a prominent politician almost totally lacking in experience in foreign affairs when he entered upon his duties in the State Department. Born in St. Louis in 1869, Colby received the A.B. degree from Williams College in 1890 and attended Columbia University Law School for one year, completing his legal studies at New York Law School

---

[1] *Current Opinion* **70** (April, 1921): pp. 438-440.

in 1892. He practiced law in New York and, among other clients, represented Samuel Clemens (Mark Twain) in reorganizing his publishing business and served as counsel in the Northern Securities anti-trust litigation. Colby was elected in 1901 to a term in the New York State Assembly, representing the Twenty-Ninth District. He was actively involved in the founding of the Progressive Party in 1912, after Theodore Roosevelt and his followers bolted the Republican convention. Colby represented William Randolph Hearst in 1915 in opposing the passage of a bill by the New York Legislature, and upon other occasions seemed to be identified with causes advocated by the newspaper tycoon. Widely admired as an effective orator, he kept small notebooks filled with quotable sayings of past and contemporary notable leaders,[2] and was one of the most popular speakers in the 1912 campaign. In 1914 he stood for election to the United States Senate on the Progressive ticket but was defeated.[3]

By 1916 Colby had evolved politically from Republican to Progressive to an Independent for Wilson; subsequently he completed the transition and ended in the Democratic Party. Colby had nominated Theodore Roosevelt at the Progressive Convention in 1916, but, when the Rough Rider declined the honor and urged Progressives to support the Republican nominee, Charles Evans Hughes, Colby led the opposition. He soon endorsed the cause of President Wilson and formed an auxiliary committee of Progressives for Wilson. He made a particularly moving speech in Wilson's behalf before the New York Press Club on June 30, that favorably impressed the President. The effort of Colby and his group apparently was a decisive factor in Wilson's

---

[2] The Papers of Bainbridge Colby (Library of Congress, Manuscripts Division).
[3] For brief biographical sketches, see John Spargo, "Bainbridge Colby," in Samuel Flagg Bemis, ed., *The American Secretaries of State and Their Diplomacy* (10 v., New York, 1927-1929) **10**: pp. 179-218; and February 29, 1920, New York *Times*.

narrow victory, particularly in western and midwestern states where Progressivism had been strongest. President Wilson came to know and esteem Colby during the course of the campaign, and after the election expressed a deep appreciation for his "generous course." [4]

Wilson offered Colby a choice of posts after the victory—Assistant Secretary of the Treasury or a federal circuit judgeship—but Colby preferred to continue his law practice in New York.[5] When the United States entered the World War, Wilson decided to reorganize the faction-ridden Shipping Board, replacing Charles Denman by E. N. Hurley as chairman. As a patriotic duty, Colby agreed to serve on the reconstituted board.[6] Some difficulty was experienced with his confirmation, since legally no more than three members of the Shipping Board could belong to the same political party. Several Republican senators argued that because Colby had supported Wilson in 1916 he would have to be classified as a Democrat, yet the board already contained three members from that party. After considerable delay and by a margin of one vote, the Commerce Committee recommended his confirmation as an Independent; the Senate granted its approval, 34 to 16.[7] A party-bolter arouses animosity even from politicians of the party benefited, and probably many Democrats secretly shared the reaction of such Republicans as former President Taft who privately referred to Colby as a "Wilson darling." [8]

On the Shipping Board, Colby helped determine and supervise rates for requisitioned private shipping. He accompanied the House War Mission to Europe in October, 1917, and participated in the establishment of the Allied

[4] Wilson to Colby, December 5, 1916, Colby Papers.
[5] Memorandum of an interview with Colby, June 30, 1930, The Papers of Ray Stannard Baker (Library of Congress, Manuscripts Division).
[6] *Ibid.;* and Wilson to Colby, July 25, and Colby to Wilson, July 28, 1917, Colby Papers.
[7] July 26 and August 9, 1917, New York *Times.*
[8] Henry F. Pringle, *The Life and Times of William Howard Taft* (2 v., New York, 1939) **2:** p. 936.

Maritime Transport Council to coordinate inter-Allied shipping allocation and supply. During his service Colby had some limited correspondence with the President on shipping problems, and he wrote Wilson a fulsome letter of congratulations on his handling of the German armistice negotiations in the fall of 1918.[9] After the Armistice, Colby wanted to return to his private practice and he submitted his resignation, but at the request of the President it was deferred until March, 1919. Despite the expressions of doubt when he had been appointed, Colby had revealed considerable ability as an administrator and had acquired a semi-diplomatic experience in shipping negotiations with the Allies.

2.

Colby's nomination as Secretary of State caused nearly universal surprise. Not long after Lansing's resignation, Joseph Tumulty, Wilson's private secretary, telephoned Colby and requested him to come to Washington. Slightly irritated by previous summons to the capital on problems dealing with shipping, Colby inquired, "Now what's up, Joe?" only to be told "I can't tell you, but come down."[10] Colby arrived at the Executive Offices on February 25 and was ushered into Wilson's presence. He found the President sitting on the South Portico, wrapped in blankets against the cold and appearing shockingly feeble and ill. Wilson asked him to accept the position of Secretary of State. Colby professed to be completely surprised by the offer; he realized his lack of experience for the position and he was reluctant to leave his law practice. Loyalty to Wilson, however, persuaded him to accept a difficult post in the last year of an expiring administration. According to Colby's

[9] Colby-Wilson exchange, October 24 and 26, 1918, Colby Papers. Wilson replied that Colby's letter had "cheered me mightily."
[10] Interview with Colby, Baker Papers.

account of the interview, he exclaimed to the President, "How shall I find words to express my appreciation?"; Wilson replied, "Colby, say you will accept." [11] After the hour-long conference, he returned to Tumulty's office and released a statement on his acceptance to the press: "I hope I shall not prove inadequate for the great duties of this new office." [12]

Although the appointment of the inexperienced Colby astonished most observers and created a political sensation surpassed recently only by Lansing's dismissal, the President's motives were understandable and defensible. Wilson greatly admired Colby's intelligence, eloquence, and writing abilities, and apparently viewed him as an excellent administrator. He had written Lansing in mid-1919 that Colby should by considered for appointment as Minister to Belgium, for he was "qualified for anything we could give him and that he would take. . . ." [13] Wilson regarded Colby as a loyal supporter, and his recent experiences with Lansing convinced him that he must have a Secretary of State whose mind "would more willingly go along" with his own. Still physically impaired, the President realized his need for a trusted assistant to write his diplomatic notes and state papers. Colby's lack of foreign policy experience was inconsequential, therefore, for Wilson intended to supply the initiative and guidance. It was possible also that Wilson thought Colby would contribute political strength in the continuing effort to ratify the peace treaty and in the 1920 presidential campaign.

Washington political circles and the nation's press generally were critical of the appointment. Colby had not been among those believed likely to replace Lansing and the news of his selection was greeted with many expressions of

[11] *Ibid.*
[12] February 26, 1920, New York *Times.*
[13] Wilson to Lansing, June 7, 1919, The Papers of Woodrow Wilson (Library of Congress, Manuscripts Division).

dismay.[14] Criticisms of Colby's frequent changes of political affiliation and his lack of diplomatic experience were mingled with disappointment that Frank Polk, Secretary of State *ad interim* since Lansing's departure, had not been given the position. Some felt that Colby was too radical, too closely identified with William Randolph Hearst, and shared the latter's Anglophobia. Massachusetts' Senator Henry Cabot Lodge, however, was reported as advising Republicans to "keep cool" on the appointment.

An editorial in the New York *Times* expressed a widely held view that while such an appointment during a critical time ordinarily would have been disturbing, the President in dismissing Lansing had emphasized his desire to replace him with someone of a more congenial and adaptable personality: "The country will assume, therefore, that the change in Secretaries involves no change in policies. The President will be his own minister of foreign affairs and Secretary Colby's mind will go along with his."[15] Consequently his appointment, although surprising and politically questionable, made little difference. The New York *Globe* found solace in the reflection that "between now and March fourth [1921] no Secretary of State is likely to do the country any irreparable harm"[16] The usually pro-administration New York *World* commented that "there could be no more complete defiance of custom and precedent."[17] One editor referred to Colby as "a decided Democrat" but one who had "only decided lately," and others criticized the appointment as "an experiment," a "diplomatic error," and a "reward for campaigning." A few editors defended the selection, however, recalling that many previous heads of the State Department had also lacked experience, while several including the Hearst chain extolled Colby as an

[14] February 26, 1920, New York *Times*.
[15] *Ibid*.
[16] *Current Opinion* 68 (April, 1920): pp. 479-482.
[17] *Literary Digest* 64 (March 13, 1920): pp. 22-23.

excellent selection, a good lawyer, administrator, and a man of courageous convictions.[18]

Members of Wilson's Cabinet were no less startled than the press by the appointment and were unenthusiastic about their new colleague. They had expected Polk to be named or, secondly, the Secretary of War, Newton D. Baker.[19] Secretary of the Treasury David F. Houston had supported Polk's candidacy, but Dr. Cary T. Grayson reported to him that Wilson needed someone with greater facility in composing state papers.[20] Tumulty also had suggested Polk's name to Mrs. Wilson, but his letter had been unanswered.[21] Eventually his colleagues apparently came to like Colby and to appreciate his merits.[22]

Senate opposition to Colby's appointment was to a large degree bipartisan, reflecting criticism of his inexperience and party irregularity. Nearly a month elapsed between Wilson's nomination and the Senate's confirmation. After an initially hostile reaction, Democratic senators upon reflection apparently decided not to oppose or interfere with the President's choice. Some began to perceive that perhaps Wilson was trying to rally progressives of both parties behind his cause.[23] William H. Anderson of the New York Anti-Saloon League announced his opposition because Colby was identified with the anti-prohibitionists. Senator

---

[18] *Ibid.*

[19] February 25, 1920, Daniels Diary, The Papers of Josephus Daniels (Library of Congress, Manuscripts Division); and Josephus Daniels, *The Wilson Era, Years of War, 1917-1921* (Chapel Hill, 1946), p. 527. James Kerney asserts that Wilson had seriously considered Baker but changed his mind because of reports that Baker had defended Lansing's role in calling meetings of the Cabinet (*The Political Education of Woodrow Wilson* [New York & London, 1926], pp. 435-436).

[20] David F. Houston, *Eight Years with Wilson's Cabinet* (2 v., Garden City, N.Y., 1926) **2**: pp. 68-69. Grayson was the White House physician. House recorded that Houston regarded Colby as particularly unfit for his position (March 2, 1920, House Diary).

[21] John M. Blum, *Joe Tumulty and the Wilson Era* (Boston, 1951), p. 237.

[22] Daniels, *Wilson Era, Years of War*, p. 527.

[23] February 27, 1920, New York *Times*. The Philadelphia *Inquirer* speculated that Wilson was trying to appeal to the old Roosevelt element for help in the next election (*Literary Digest* **64** [March, 1920]: pp. 22-23).

Lodge pronounced the appointment one of the most important ever made, in view of the poor health of both the President and the Vice President and the fact that the Secretary of State would be next in line of succession.[24] The Senate Foreign Relations Committee insisted upon a full hearing and held closed sessions on the appointment. Obviously the committee felt no sense of urgency. At one session the Chief of Army Intelligence testified, causing rumors, though apparently his remarks about Colby were not derogatory. Colby appeared before the committee on March 18 and made a long statement in defense of his record, described by the Democratic leader, Gilbert M. Hitchcock, as a "complete knockout" over his opponents.[25] The committee favorably reported the nomination, without a recorded vote, and the Senate confirmed it on March 22 in executive session also without a recorded vote.[26] Only a handful of senators had been present and a few nays were expressed in the voice vote. Polk's *ad interim* appointment, legally non-renewable, had expired a week earlier, leaving the department technically without a head. Colby took the oath of office without ceremony on March 23, 1920.

3.

Colby admittedly lacked experience for his new responsibilities but, as one editor had pointed out, that also had been

[24] Spargo, "Colby," p. 197.
[25] March 11 and 18, 1920, New York *Times*. Although Lansing sent Colby a brief and formal letter of congratulations on February 28 (Lansing Papers), he apparently tried to stimulate opposition to Colby's confirmation by reminding Chandler Anderson, a lawyer close to the Republican leadership, of Colby's former connections with the Standard Oil Company, which he related to the role of the Shipping Board in the *Imperator* controversy (February 27, 1920, Anderson Diary, Papers of Chandler P. Anderson [Library of Congress, Manuscripts Division]). Colby disposed of his private interests in the Inglaterra Mining Company (Colby to Henry M. Anderson of New York City, March 20, 1920, Colby Papers).
[26] March 20 and 23, 1920, New York *Times*.

true of such able predecessors as Richard Olney and Elihu Root. The increasing importance of foreign affairs to the republic seemed to indicate the need for greater preparation, however, as much of the comment on Colby's appointment had emphasized. In the years prior to 1920, Colby occasionally had spoken publicly on aspects of America's foreign relations. In 1914, reflecting his identification with the Irish-American cause and his apparent Anglophobia, Colby had spoken at Carnegie Hall in New York City in opposition to repeal of tolls exemptions for American coastal shipping using the Panama Canal. He had unflatteringly criticized President Wilson as nervous and Ambassador to Britain Walter Hines Page as an "arch comedian" for advocating repeal. His harshest remarks, however, had been reserved for Secretary Bryan: the nation's honor did not need to be saved by such men as Root or "the pathetic futilities of the itinerant Chautauquan who occupies but does not fill the office of Secretary of State." [27] Subsequently Colby had helped organize a non-partisan committee, known as the "Provisional Committee for the Preservation of American Rights in the Panama Canal," to oppose what he described as the "unpatriotic attitude" of the administration.[28] Colby seemed to reveal an alarming tendency, at least in the view of many observers, to unpredictable and unrestrained activity.[29]

As most other prominent citizens, Colby evidenced a greatly quickened interest in foreign affairs after the beginning of the European war. He advocated a firm policy during the *Lusitania* crisis and was critical of Wilson and Bryan for their failure to follow "brave words" with decisive measures:

> The American people have always stood by the President. But they expect the President to stand by them. The dignity of the flag,

[27] March 21, 1914, *ibid.*
[28] April 9 and 10, 1914, *ibid.*
[29] February 29, 1920, *ibid.*

and the honor of the nation are in his keeping. . . . While the people expect him to be deliberate, they do not expect him to waver and hesitate. While the responsibility is great, they expect it to be met unflinchingly and borne cheerfully. . . .[30]

Colby participated in the movement for greater military preparedness to defend American rights and interests. He spoke at a meeting convened in June, 1915, by the National Security League on "Peace and Preparation," and later before a group appointed by the Governor of New York, known as the New York State Committee on National Defense. The latter body adopted a resolution, offered by Colby, that strongly recommended defensive preparations to the attention of the President and Congress.[31] He was selected as a member of the Congress of the World Court League in 1916, and addressed an appeal to the meeting for military defensive measures pending the achievement of a rational alternative to war.[32] The cause of Irish freedom, politically important in a state such as New York, also evoked his aggressive championship in 1916. He condemned the execution of Roger Casement and other Irish patriots involved in the Easter Rebellion, and declared that Great Britain had no legal foundation for its control of the Emerald Isle.[33] Colby also was involved in the League to Enforce Peace, and served as an intermediary when Wilson urged its director, William H. Taft, not to embarrass the administration by drafting a detailed plan on the proposed world league.[34]

Representing the Shipping Board, Colby sailed in the fall of 1917 with Colonel House, Admiral Benson, Vance McCormick of the War Trade Board, and the Assistant Secretary of the Treasury, Oscar T. Crosby, aboard the cruiser

[30] Letter to the Editor, May 11, 1915, *ibid.*
[31] June 16 and November 4, 1915, *ibid.*
[32] May 3, 1916, *ibid.*
[33] January 7, 1917; and sketch of February 29, 1920, *ibid.*
[34] Taft to Colby, March 18, 1918, Colby Papers; and Pringle, *Taft* **2**: pp. 936-937.

Huntington for a special war mission to the Allies. According to Colby's account, just before he departed President Wilson told him, "Now be an American. Our men only last about six months in England and then they become Anglicized." [35] Unlike Walter Hines Page and others, Colby undoubtedly did not require such an exhortation. The mission has been described as of decisive importance in the work of coordination and concentration of war effort which led to the Allied triumph. It apparently also was a heady experience. Upon their return to the United States, Colby facetiously wrote House that they needed to get back to their "own level" again after such intimate association with kings and nobles.[36]

As Wilson began to mature plans for a league of nations, Colby became an enthusiastic supporter of the cause. In an article published early in 1919, he argued that a return to a balance of power system, advocated by the French Premier Georges Clemenceau, was inadequate to maintain peace; Wilson's concept of a community of power was "the only escape from the organized rivalries of nations. . . ."

> One view [Clemenceau's] is old, oft tried, and history has yet to record an instance in which it has proved successful as a means of averting war. The other is new. It may fail, but it has at least the relative prestige of not already having failed. . . .[37]

Colby reviewed for his readers the history of the Congress of Vienna and the Holy Alliance to buttress his interpretation. He spoke at a meeting of the Atlantic Congress for a League of Nations, in February in New York City, along with Taft and others, and joined in the chorus of approval of the formation and membership in a league as indispensable for world peace. Colby hit vigorously at Wilson's senatorial critics:

---

[35] As quoted in Kerney, *Political Education of Woodrow Wilson*, pp. 383-384.
[36] Charles Seymour, *American Diplomacy during the World War* (Baltimore, 1934), pp. 232-233, 239; and *The Intimate Papers of Colonel House* (4 v., Boston & New York, 1926-1928) **3**: p. 292.
[37] January 12, 1919, New York *Times*.

I sometimes wonder on what kind of reading the Senatorial mind is nourished. The denunciation which various Senators hurl from day to day at the mere suggestion of an organized world peace, seems to me to be characterized by a vast illiteracy, a complete lack of touch with the sober and responsible thought of our own people and of our heroic allies.[38]

Opponents who talked of preserving America's sovereign freedom ignored the fact that it had passed for both the Allies and the United States, for victory had been achieved in the war only by the concerted effort of all. After Wilson returned to Europe from his brief trip to the United States, Colby with the President's approval spoke in defense of the Covenant at St. Louis on April 4, in what Tumulty described as a necessary attempt to silence critics such as Senator James A. Reed of Missouri (D).[39]

4.

Despite the rash of resignations after the Peace Treaty with Germany had been signed, the State Department was efficiently administered under Colby and its morale apparently greatly improved. In contrast to the ailing Lansing, he was a good administrator and his excellent relations with the White House eliminated much of the previous uncertainty in the work of the department.[40] William Phillips, Assistant Secretary of State, left in March for his post as Minister to the Netherlands, and his office remained vacant until the Harding administration.[41] Another Assistant Secretary, Breckinridge Long, resigned in June, to be replaced by a New York lawyer and banker, V. S. Merle-

---

[38] February 6, 1919, *ibid*.

[39] Tumulty arranged the address and got from Wilson a denial of any secret protocol attached to the Covenant (Tumulty to Wilson, March 25, and Wilson's reply, March 27, 1919, Wilson Papers; and April 5, 1919, New York *Times*).

[40] Graham M. Stuart, *The Department of State: A History of Its Organization Procedure and Personnel* (New York, 1949), pp. 254-255.

[41] Colby-Wilson exchange, April 12 and 13, 1920, Wilson Papers.

Smith, a questionable appointment in view of his responsibility for general administrative functions. At Wilson's desire, Norman H. Davis was brought from the Treasury Department to concentrate on reparations problems. The President had greatly admired Davis' work at Paris and viewed him as possessing an unrivaled knowledge of the intricacies of international relations—probably also he appreciated the inexperienced Colby's need for expert guidance. The new Secretary was also favorably impressed with Davis.[42] A high-ranking post was made available when Polk decided to resign as Undersecretary of State. Probably he had been disappointed and hurt at not succeeding Lansing, but his health was declining and he had warned Lansing earlier that he would soon have to leave the department.[43] Colby wrote the President that Polk had "behaved towards me in the most high-born and generous way, and has shown the finest conceivable attitude toward his work. . . ."[44] When he left on June 15, Davis was appointed Undersecretary. Although he was Wilson's choice, Davis worked harmoniously with Colby and was responsible for much of the actual direction of the department.

During his brief tenure, Colby established good relations with the press and with the business community. Although he excluded from his daily news conferences two representatives of radical and Socialist newspapers, who had charged that the Secretary deliberately manipulated information relating to foreign affairs, it was generally agreed that he was more liberal and frank in the release of news than had been several of his predecessors.[45] Colby supported the movement for departmental and foreign-service reorganization

[42] Wilson to Colby, April 2, and Colby to Wilson, April 10, 1920, *ibid.*
[43] Allan Nevins, ed., *The Letters and Journal of Brand Whitlock* (2 v., New York, 1936) **2**: p. 599; and Wilson to Polk, April 15, and Polk to Wilson, April 16, 1920, Wilson Papers.
[44] Colby to Wilson, April 24, 1920, Wilson Papers.
[45] September 30, 1920, New York *Times*. The two newsmen were Paul Hanna of the New York *Call* and Lawrence Todd of the Fargo *Courier-News*, allegedly representing approximately one hundred radical and Socialist organs.

launched earlier by Lansing. His request for the use of technical trade experts to enable the United States to compete commercially with its rivals, together with the department's firm position toward British attempts to monopolize oil exploitation in its Mesopotamian mandate, was interpreted as indicating an aggressive attitude by the United States in defense of foreign trade.[46]

Colby's relationship with Wilson was very close and warm. To a large degree he occupied the intimate position formerly held by House, although in contrast with the latter his role was confined primarily to foreign affairs. As Wilson's "official" biographer, R. S. Baker, later wrote perceptively, Colby was "an extremely brilliant, but somewhat erratic man, a gentleman, gifted [with] a rare facility of expression, both in conversation and oratory, faculties which always attracted Woodrow Wilson." [47] Soon after Colby had taken the oath of office, the President expressed to him "my hearty satisfaction that you are in charge and that we are to have intimate counsel with one another. . . ." [48] Particularly in view of his physical condition, Wilson was grateful for a counselor able to write state papers measuring up to his high standards. In a confidential interview with a reporter in September, 1920, Wilson revealed his satisfaction:

. . . I can tell you that for the first time, I have a man who can write a note for me. You know, heretofore, I have always had to write them myself. But the note on the Polish situation was written by Colby. It was his note not mine. He is a great man.[49]

After Mrs. Wilson demurred, Wilson hastened to add that

[46] December 20 and 27, 1920, New York *Times*.
[47] Interview with Colby, R. S. Baker Papers. Baker concluded that Colby would have had an even more distinguished career if his brilliance had been more disciplined.
[48] Wilson to Colby, March 25, 1920, Colby Papers.
[49] Confidential Interview by William W. Hawkins of Scripps-Howard, September 27, 1920, copy sent to Colby on August 11, 1933, Colby Papers. Wilson commented to the reporter that Bryan had the "strangest mind" of any man he had ever known, while "Lansing wasn't even true."

he was referring only to the phraseology of that note relating to Soviet Russia and Poland, for he and Colby had discussed it several times and the ideas were those of the President.

Colby fully reciprocated Wilson's admiration and affection. He was exactly the type of loyal supporter that the President had always sought and whom he could fully trust. Although Wilson was obviously still physically impaired, Colby found him to be alert, with no diminution of his old clarity and mental perceptiveness. The President continued to lean on his wife for physical support, but he resumed Cabinet meetings on April 14 and steadily increased his role in the direction of the executive government. Exaggerating his recovery, Colby declared to a reporter in the summer of 1920 that the President was "doing more and better work than any man in Washington...."[50] Colby and the other department heads did try to shorten their interviews with Wilson and to come quickly to the point in order to avoid imposing unnecessary strains on him.[51] Care also had to be taken not to arouse the suspicions of the President, who was impatient at the protective restrictions previously imposed on his correspondence during his illness. He instructed both Colby and Navy Secretary Josephus Daniels in August, 1920, to communicate thereafter with him directly and not through third persons such as Tumulty or Grayson.[52]

Colby quickly became immersed in the continuing struggle for Senate approval of the Versailles Treaty. Any inclination he might have had toward compromise with the Republican opposition was speedily abandoned when Wilson indicated an obstinate refusal to consider concilia-

[50] August 4, 1920, New York *Times*.
[51] Bainbridge Colby, *The Close of Woodrow Wilson's Administration and the Final Years* (New York, 1930), p. 16. A reprint of an address by Colby to the Missouri Historical Society at St. Louis, April 28, 1930.
[52] Wilson to Daniels, August 28, 1920, Daniels Papers; and Wilson to Colby, August 28, 1920, Wilson Papers.

tory moves, despite the Senate's failure to approve the Treaty on March 19, 1920. Hitchcock wrote Colby from Atlanta about a possible new effort to obtain Senate approval with moderate reservations. He recommended that the Treaty be resubmitted to the Senate with "some well drawn reservations of an interpretative character," after the approval of the Allied governments had been obtained; in his opinion such a step would reassert presidential leadership, favorably impress the public, and place the burden of obstructionism on Lodge.[53] Wilson expressed keen disappointment that the Senator wanted to return to the point previously reached and passed: "At present the dead treaty lies very heavy on the consciences of those who killed it and I am content to let it lie there until those consciences are either crushed or awakened." [54] He might be wrong, he admitted, and he expressed a willingness to allow Colby to try to dissuade him from that course of prolonged deadlock. Colby apparently made no such effort. At the meeting of the Cabinet on April 20, Daniels recorded that the President spoke "vigorously (if not viciously)" about the men whom he claimed had killed the Treaty, and he refused to accept Postmaster General Albert S. Burleson's advice that he place the responsibility squarely on the Senate by informing the opposition precisely what reservations he would accept. "It is dead," said Wilson, "and lies over there. Every morning I put flowers on its grave." [55]

The President's reaction hardly accorded with Colby's subsequent statement that he had never heard Wilson speak with bitterness about his opponents in the Treaty fight.[56]

[53] Hitchcock to Colby, March 29, 1920, Colby Papers.
[54] Colby to Wilson, April 1, and Wilson to Colby, April 2, 1920, *ibid.*
[55] April 20, 1920, Daniels Diary.
[56] Colby, *Close of Wilson's Administration*, p. 13. Illustrative of Wilson's capacity for hate, he wrote Davis on December 9, 1920, that Herbert Hoover, a wartime administration official but now a Republican defector, "is no friend of mind [*sic*] and I do not care to do anything to assist him in any way in any undertaking whatever" (Wilson Papers).

Responding to the President's mood, Colby wrote him an effusive letter that personal contact with him at the Cabinet meeting had had a "tonic effect" on them all: "I see your point of view on the Treaty, and that is all I want to see. I know you are right, and I'm tugging at the leash for the fight to begin," for "Your inflexible courage must eventually carry everything before it." [57] Such uncritical and devoted adherence to Wilson's views stood in sharp contrast to the role played by the more independent and critical-minded Lansing, and helps explain why the President was so pleased with his new Secretary of State. Colby did include in his letter a closely reasoned memorandum by Norman Davis that argued for action to clarify public opinion by putting the responsibility squarely on the Senate. Davis suggested that the President notify the Allied governments that the Senate's criticism of the Treaty centered on Article X, the Monroe Doctrine, and the six British votes in the League Assembly; if the Allies found reservations on these points acceptable, Wilson would declare his readiness to resubmit the Treaty with appropriate changes. These interpretative reservations would dissipate the general impression that the President was not conciliatory and would draw a clear issue with the opposition. Since many senators were then in a more compromising mood and were anxious to adjourn for the forthcoming political conventions, Davis believed that Wilson's position would be greatly strengthened. Although Wilson indicated that he would give careful reflection to the memorandum, nothing resulted. The tone of his reply to Colby's letter, however, was most flattering to the Secretary: "I read your letter . . . with the deepest appreciation. Just what I expected and hoped for is happening. Our minds are traveling the same road and are keeping step,

[57] Colby to Wilson, April 24, 1920 (enclosing a memorandum by Norman Davis), Wilson Papers.

and this is wholly delightful to me." [58] It hardly needs to be pointed out that it was the road to defeat and an isolationist-inclined America.

Colby gave a number of addresses advocating ratification of the Treaty without reservations. He vigorously defended Wilson's position, but probably without winning many new adherents to the cause. He assured his audience at the 48th annual Press Club dinner that the President was rapidly recovering his former vigor:

> He is neither cowed nor is his valiant spirit bent by these contemptible attacks that have been made upon him in such an unsportsmanlike spirit through the months of the Winter. Like ravening wolves, his assailants have girded at him by day and by night, but the people, whom he loves and serves . . . have yet to speak.
>
> . . . .
>
> I venture the prediction . . . that as the people speak there will be a notable exodus of conspicuous gentlemen who have had it all their own way for a little while.[59]

Undoubtedly Colby's remarks were most pleasing to Wilson and expressed his own belief that the people were still behind his policy, but it was questionable statesmanship and poor politics in the climate of 1920.

Colby conferred with Senators Hitchcock and Oscar W. Underwood to block the Republican-sponsored Knox resolution for a separate peace with Germany.[60] A few days later he spoke to the Chicago Bar Association, to argue that the United States was no longer isolated if it ever had been. Colby declared that history revealed that overt challenges to the Monroe Doctrine had been averted not by

---

[58] Wilson to Colby, April 26, 1920, *ibid*. At the Cabinet meeting on May 4, Wilson reiterated opposition to returning the Treaty to the Senate with reservations he could accept, and he declared that he would veto a Republican resolution to end the state of war without approving the Versailles Treaty (Daniels Diary).

[59] May 2, 1920, New York *Times*.

[60] May 5, 1920, *ibid*.

the prestige and power of the United States alone, but with the assistance of the European balance of power that had restrained overly-ambitious European states from trying to expand in the New World. The great question before the American people was what role the United States should have in the restoration of order in Europe, and Colby hailed the League as "the law of the world today." [61] As for the alleged prohibitions by Washington and Jefferson against foreign entanglements, Colby pointed out that those two statesmen had not been adverse to alliances for temporary or specific purposes, and obviously had not intended to speak for a future America and its problems.

Part of Wilson's strategy for converting the 1920 election into a "solemn referendum" on the League apparently was to seek nomination by the Democratic Convention for a third term in the presidency. No one else could better dramatize the key issue as he saw it, and Colby lent himself fully to the plan. Wilson declined to remove himself as a potential nominee particularly since, as he told Grayson, the convention might deadlock over the nomination of someone else and compel him to run again.[62] When the Republican Convention nominated Warren G. Harding, Colby joined other Democrats in expressing his delight: "From the standpoint of the Democratic Party, this nomination of Mr. Harding is a very admirable one, because it tends to clarify and emphasize every issue between the two

---

[61] May 14, 1920, *ibid.*

[62] Cary T. Grayson, *Woodrow Wilson, An Intimate Memoir* (New York, 1960), pp. 114-117. See Wesley Bagby, "Woodrow Wilson, a Third Term, and the Solemn Referendum," *Amer. Hist. Rev.* 60 (1955): pp. 567-575; and his *The Road to Normalcy: the Presidential Campaign and Election of 1920* (Baltimore, 1962), pp. 54-63, 117-120. Because of domestic political factors, Colby at first thought that Wilson should not comply with the request of the Secretary-General of the League of Nations that the President issue the call for the first session of the Assembly; Wilson agreed. Subsequently Davis and Colby reversed themselves and advised that he should act, and the notice was sent from the White House for the first meeting. Colby to Wilson, June 11 and Davis to Wilson, July 6, 1920, Wilson Papers; and Colby to Wilson, June 17 and 19, 1920, Colby Papers.

parties." [63] He professed optimism about the outcome of the election with the opposition led by a "stand-patter." Colby was selected as a delegate from the District of Columbia to the Democratic Convention. He was given to understand that the President wanted him to attend and to serve as the permanent chairman of the Convention. He inquired on June 18 if Wilson still desired that, or if a possible struggle over Colby's selection as chairman might not "initiate conflict which may have an effect on more important questions before the Convention?" [64] The President replied affirmatively and expressed the conviction that Colby at the San Francisco Convention would be of the greatest service to the cause.[65]

Other Democratic politicians also definitely got the impression that Wilson sought a third nomination. Colby conferred with the President for an hour prior to his departure on June 21 for San Francisco. What transpired is unknown, but although Colby denied to reporters that he had ever discussed the matter with the President, his subsequent actions indicated that he believed that Wilson wanted the nomination.[66] A decade later, he admitted to R. S. Baker that he had almost nominated Wilson at San Francisco. As Baker noted after the interview, "Colby worshipped Wilson, and still does." [67] At the convention Colby sharply challenged remarks by Bryan and spoke in behalf of ratification of the Treaty without reservations. In an extemporaneous speech, Colby noted that Bryan (who had proposed letting Congress end the state of war by majority vote) called the Versailles Treaty the "best treaty that anybody could possibly have made. He says there is not another man in the world who could have brought back a

---

[63] June 13, 1920, New York *Times*.
[64] Colby to Wilson, June 18, 1920, Wilson Papers.
[65] Wilson to Colby, June 19, 1920, *ibid*. Senator Joseph T. Robinson of Arkansas was chosen permanent chairman of the convention.
[66] June 22 and 23, 1920, New York *Times*.
[67] Interview with Colby, R. S. Baker Papers.

better treaty. . . . Well, then, for God's sake, let's ratify it." [68] Exhorting the nation to close its ears to "the siren voices" of the reservationists and amenders, Colby urged that the United States ratify the Treaty as a great step toward a better world. He wired the President on July 2 that the Convention was prepared to renominate him and he proposed, unless otherwise instructed, to place Wilson's name before the Convention. The "outstanding characteristic of the Convention is the unanimity and fervor of feeling for you," he reported, though he admitted that Bryan was a "watchful, tireless enemy." [69] He planned to ask for a suspension of the rules, to place Wilson's name before the body. Word from the White House to Colby was that his plan was not unacceptable to Wilson. When Daniels and other administration leaders learned of Colby's intention, however, they agreed that Wilson's health was unequal to the burden and managed after some hours of argument to dissuade Colby from acting.[70] A very disappointed and reluctant Colby was compelled to send Wilson a second telegram stating that factional lines in the Convention were so tightly drawn that it was inadvisable to put his name into nomination. Apparently Wilson was greatly disappointed and thereafter was reserved in his attitude toward some of the Democratic leaders, especially Burleson. The nomination went to Governor James M. Cox of Ohio, with Franklin D. Roosevelt as his running mate.

After the Convention, Colby continued to speak in support of immediate membership in the League. He criticized as unworkable the Root plan, reportedly under consideration by certain Republicans close to Harding, for the substitution of a World Court for the League, and he implied that the Court could not be separated from the

[68] June 28 and August 8, 1920, New York *Times*.
[69] Colby to Wilson, July 2, 1920, Wilson Papers.
[70] Daniels, *Wilson Era, Years of War*, pp. 555-557.

League project.[71] In a series of speeches made in the midwest, Colby flailed at the opposition. In St. Louis on October 14 he defended the linking of the Treaty and the Covenant as not a deliberate Wilson plan but virtually unavoidable at Paris, and he charged Harding with inconsistency in earlier stating that he opposed only Wilson's version of the League but then at Senator William E. Borah's insistence condemning membership in any league. With scathing wit, Colby exclaimed of Harding's public shifts: "At last we have him. . . . He has at last severed his moorings with the nation's conscience and aspirations. He is drifting out into the sea of opportunism unchartered by principle or high purpose." [72] In Springfield, Illinois, the Secretary attacked as impractical Harding's vague references in an address at Indianapolis to negotiating a new league of nations; Article XX of the Covenant, Colby pointed out, precluded members from entering into or negotiating "his peculiar and amorphous association or league or what not." Who would Harding find to negotiate with, except for the defeated countries and a few others that did not belong to the League: "there is no alternative to membership in the League except complete isolation for the United States—isolation against the world." [73] In two addresses in Chicago, Colby condemned efforts to arouse ethnic minority groups against the Treaty and membership in the League as sinister and irresponsible: "I sometimes feel that the Republican Party is engaged in an effort to Balkanize the electorate." [74] Harding should be embarrassed, Colby declared, by the presence of wartime German

[71] September 17, 1920, New York *Times*.
[72] October 15, 1920, *ibid*.
[73] October 16, 1920, *ibid*. Borah, Republican leader of the "Irreconcilables," in a speech in New York agreed with Colby that if Europe could not have the present League there would be no league at all. He objected to the Covenant as a repudiation of Washington's Farewell Address, and thought any Harding-proposed league would also amount to the same thing (October 17, 1920, *ibid*.).
[74] October 17, 1920, *ibid*.

supporters in his camp. In contrast, the Secretary described the Democratic Party as "an American party," appealing to Americans on American issues and welcoming the foreign-born but only as new Americans. Perhaps Colby, an astute politician, was trying to trump Republican minority tactics with a Democratic nativist appeal. Root's criticism in an address at Carnegie Hall that Article X substituted coercive force for moral suasion and amounted to a perpetuation of control by the victors was refuted by Colby as an "inversion of the truth." "Root is in favor of going in [to the League]," the Secretary quipped, "but with his coat buttoned up to his chin, one hand clenching his reservations, and the other the privilege of withdrawal." [75]

Returning to the capital outwardly confident, Colby predicted a Democratic victory at the polls and ratification of the Treaty.[76] In a thoughtful interview with William H. Crawford, a New York *Times* reporter, the Secretary pointed out that the United States in fact never had been isolated from European politics and twice, in 1812 and 1917, had been pulled into great wars despite its wishes. Only by entering the League could the American people be assured of peace in the future.

No doubt Colby had entertained partisan audiences with his flashing wit and biting satire, but the effects on the general electorate were questionable. The mood of the American people still appeared to be favorable to membership in the League but with reservations curtailing the degree of American commitment and preserving as much diplomatic freedom as possible. The expressed willingness of Cox and Roosevelt to accept some changes was a far more realistic approach, but Colby was constrained by his official position to an uncompromising attitude. He apparently agreed completely with Wilson that nothing else would suffice.

[75] October 23, 1920, *ibid.*
[76] October 27 and 31, 1920, *ibid.*

After Harding's sweeping victory in the solemn referendum, Colby tried to console Wilson: "I am bowed under the weight of disappointment today, but my thoughts turn to you—solicitously and tenderly."[77] He hoped that the President was not depressed, and wisely attributed the defeat to a complex of causes that could not dim the luster of Wilson's leadership. In identical replies to Colby and Newton Baker, Wilson expressed warm pleasure and reassurance: "What every thoughtful man most deeply and earnestly desires is loyal and generous friendship. This you have given me in extraordinary measure and quality, and I am greatly enriched. More complete satisfaction or reward I could not desire."[78] The weary and disappointed President requested Colby to draft the annual Thanksgiving Proclamation, for though he claimed he had "no resentment in my heart I find myself very much put to it to frame a proper proclamation."[79] Colby's first effort failed to conceal his own great disappointment at the results of the election, and Wilson asked him to try again. Colby hoped that the bland generalities of his second effort would "satisfy even [the] 'America first' " sentiment of many citizens, and Wilson approved it.[80]

Although some proposals were made for a renewed effort, the Treaty was dead. On November 9 the Cabinet debated whether Wilson should resubmit it to the Senate, with Colby favoring such action against the skepticism of Daniels and others.[81] Federal Circuit Judge George W. Anderson of Boston recommended that Wilson resubmit it with a statement that in view of the election results he would accept such modifications as the Senate thought wise;

---

[77] Colby to Wilson, November 3, 1920, Wilson Papers.
[78] Wilson to Colby, November 7, 1920, *ibid.*
[79] Wilson to Colby, November 6, 1920, *ibid.*
[80] Wilson to Colby, November 10, Colby to Wilson, November 11, and Wilson's reply, November 12, 1920, *ibid.*
[81] November 9, 1920, Daniels Diary.

in that way, the burden would be placed on the Senate, as the Republicans allegedly feared, and it might be possible to get a better treaty than the next administration could obtain. Colby may have been attracted by the proposal, but he sent Anderson's letter to the President without any comment. Wilson expressed continued opposition, for in his view the Lodge Reservations had not been made in good faith and were intended to nullify the Treaty.[82] He asked for Colby's opinion but there is no record of his response. Colby was too loyal and too astute to support a course to which his chief was obviously opposed.

[82] Wilson to Colby, November 20, 1920, Colby Papers.

II. Europe: Discord with the Allies

THE BRIEFNESS of his tenure in office and the deadlock between the President and Congress over the Treaty of Versailles did not allow Colby many opportunities for significant achievement in regard to European affairs. Not only non-ratification of the German Peace Treaty but Wilson's own changing attitudes toward Europe after the peace conference sharply limited the scope of American diplomacy. Of course, the President had been under few if any illusions about the Allies' war goals during the recent war and at the Paris conference. Now doubly embittered by his domestic frustrations and the apparent willingness of America's cobelligerents to ignore her in determining the remaining details of the postwar settlement, Wilson seemed increasingly disillusioned and on occasion loath to play even that diminished role in European affairs still possible despite the Senate's failure to approve the Versailles Treaty.

Colby was a dedicated Wilsonian internationalist. In East Asia, where American involvement long antedated World War I, the State Department under his direction was able to exert a vigorous leadership for the United States, based on a close understanding with the British government and aimed at persuading Japan to cooperate in creating a stable order for the region of the Pacific. But, largely because of Wilson's own attitudes, the record was more mixed in regard to European affairs, characterized by continued interest in some problems and non-participation in others, and all within an official climate of growing resentment and suspicion of Allied motives.

1.

American policy toward Europe had been undergoing a gradual change for some months prior to Colby's secretaryship. A combination of diminished interest in the work of the peace conference remaining after the German treaty had been completed and considerations of political strategy in the struggle with the Senate explained the decision to recall the American peace commissioners from Paris in late 1919. Suspicions of Allied purposes, especially those of France, also were involved in that decision. After Wilson and Lansing had left the peace conference in mid-1919, four commissioners had remained to represent the United States: Colonel House, General Tasker H. Bliss. Henry White, and Lansing's replacement as the head of the mission, Frank Polk. House had soon left also, in ill-health and complaining that "It is perfectly useless my being in Paris at this time. It is practically deserted as far as the directing powers of the government[s] are concerned." [1] After the Senate's first rejection of the Versailles Treaty, in the vote on November 19, 1919, Secretary Lansing concurred with one of the Democratic leaders in the Senate, Oscar Underwood of Alabama, that an immediate recall of the remaining American commissioners would emphasize Republican responsibility for the unfortunate situation. Informed by Mrs. Wilson, the zealous guardian of her husband's sick room, that the President wanted the mission to remain, Lansing wrote a lengthy explanation of the reasons for a prompt recall. Terminating American representation at the remaining work of the peace conference, by displeasing businessmen interested in a speedy restoration of peace and trade, would put pressure on obstructionist senators. Moreover,

[1] House to Lansing, September 15, 19, and 26, 1919, *Papers Relating to the Foreign Relations of the United States: The Paris Peace Conference* (13 v., Washington, 1942-1947) **11**: pp. 644, 647-649.

Lansing thought that the present business before the peace conference was not too significant in terms of American interests.[2] Mrs. Wilson relayed the President's approval and Lansing notified Polk that he and the other commissioners were being withdrawn immediately. There would be no American representation on any of the commissions provided by the Versailles Treaty, except for the Reparations Commission, and for the present the American Ambassador to France, Hugh C. Wallace, should not sit even as an observer at the peace conference.[3]

The French government was greatly distressed. Polk pled for some concessions to the work of the conference and European opinion. French Ambassador Jules Jusserand protested to Lansing on November 29 that the department's action would encourage Germany to refuse or delay in fulfilling Armistice conditions and the signing of the protocol to implement the Versailles Treaty. Although he agreed with the Secretary that it was time to leave, Polk urged the delay of a few days, from the scheduled December 1 to the ninth, in order to clear up remaining problems and to assuage French apprehensions. Premier Clemenceau, Polk related, feared the effects of a precipitate American withdrawal.[4] Britain also supported the French position. Lansing wrote Wilson that, although he appreciated France's wish to continue the Supreme Council of the peace conference, it no longer was effective and the American delegates should return:

Of course the French desire the Council to continue because, as it is now constituted, M. Clemenceau practically dominates it, and is using . . . such power as it still possesses to carry out French

[2] Lansing to Wilson, November 20, 1919, Wilson Papers; November 20, 21, and December 4, 1919, Lansing Desk Diary; and *For. Rel., Paris Peace Conference* 11: pp. 669-671.
[3] *For. Rel., Paris Peace Conference* 11: pp. 672-673.
[4] November 29, 1919, Lansing Desk Diary; *For. Rel., Paris Peace Conference*, 11: pp. 673-674; and *Papers Relating to the Foreign Relations of the United States, 1919* (2 v., Washington, 1936) 1: pp. 23-26.

policies in Europe which . . . will be likely to cause the overthrow of the present German Government, a fact which would be most unfortunate.[5]

He thought, however, that Germany might balk in signing the protocol, and advised that every effort should be made to obtain favorable Senate action on the Treaty. Wilson agreed that the decision to leave must be implemented, although a delay until December 9 was permissible.[6]

Although Clemenceau was "tremendously pleased" at the postponement of the departure, according to Polk he was deeply disturbed at the apparent lack of an arrangement for an American presence in observing the German situation: "He said that it appeared as if France were being abandoned." There was much "bitter criticism" of America in British and French circles, Polk reported, and "It is said that it is impossible to rely on the United States."[7] A few days earlier, Polk and his colleagues had recommended that General Bliss be left at Paris until Germany signed the protocol, thereby relieving French fears, but Lansing acting for the President had refused. Lansing informed Polk on December 6 that he might explain to Clemenceau that the American withdrawal reflected not only the effects of the Senate's action on November 19 but also the view of many Americans that the Supreme Council of the peace conference was trying to impose a dictatorship by the victorious great powers on Europe, an unjustifiable procedure in which America should not further participate.[8] Personally, Lansing thought that Germany would sign the protocol if certain modifications were made in regard to the surrender of materials demanded in compensation for the scuttling of

---

[5] Lansing to Wilson, December 1, 1919, and Mrs. Wilson's reply of the same date, *For. Rel., Paris Peace Conference* **11**: pp. 680-682.

[6] *For. Rel., 1919* **1**: p. 26.

[7] Polk to Lansing, December 5, 1920, *For. Rel., Paris Peace Conference* **11**: p. 691.

[8] *Ibid* **11**: pp. 685-686, 691-692.

the German fleet by its crews at Scapa Flow, changes that he deemed advisable.

After receipt of still another cable from Polk, regretting the precipitancy of the American departure and expressing the need for someone such as the American Ambassador to France to represent the United States in the completion of work on the Hungarian and Roumanian treaties, Lansing wrote Wilson and reluctantly advised that Ambassador Wallace be designated as an observer at the conference. Mrs. Wilson replied that the President concurred, and Wallace was instructed accordingly. "I desire...," Lansing informed the Ambassador, "that you take no action and express no opinion on any subjects discussed" by the Supreme Council but report fully to the State Department for its decisions.[9] Wallace observed the work of the peace conference in the final phases of the peacemaking, sitting in what was called the Conference or Council of Ambassadors.

The decision to withdraw the mission was understandable politics, and probably did have some effect in increasing popular pressures on the Senate, as Lansing and the Democratic strategists had hoped. But the popular mood apparently also favored compromise on the Treaty by the President, which he adamantly opposed as noted earlier. Unfortunately, withdrawal was an extreme weapon that could only be used once, and it might have been far more effective to have postponed its application, meanwhile pointing out to the public the implications of the Senate's actions. More importantly, withdrawal represented a kind of victory for the "Irreconcilables" or isolationist opponents of the League in the Senate and the country. Withdrawal did not mean the cessation of all interest by the United States government in Europe, of course, but it did render it more difficult to exert a decisive influence and had the

[9] *Ibid.* **11**: pp. 693-698.

effect of heightening suspicions and misunderstandings of the Allies. Such was the legacy that Colby inherited when he succeeded Lansing.

2.

In the month before Colby's appointment as Secretary of State was confirmed, alarming reports flowed into Washington that France sought to extend its control over prostrate Germany. The American observer on the Rhineland High Commission, Pierrepont B. Noyes, reported that France was exerting both overt and covert pressure on the commission for a strong policy of extensive and, he thought, unnecessary controls of German transportation and economic activity in the demilitarized and occupied Rhineland.[10] Wilson requested Polk, the *ad interim* Secretary of State, to intimate to Ambassador Jusserand that France must expect to face strong American opposition if it persisted in trying to exploit every technical deficiency by Germany in carrying out the armistice and peace terms as an excuse to increase military controls. He feared that France sought permanent control of the Rhineland, thereby contributing to a probable future war.[11] Polk also instructed the American diplomats in the Allied capitals that the United States was opposed to excessive demands for reparations.[12]

When Communist-instigated uprisings occurred in the demilitarized Ruhr, the German government urgently requested permission to send a small number of troops into

[10] *Papers Relating to the Foreign Relations of the United States, 1920* (3 v., Washington, 1935-1936) **2**: pp. 289-296.
[11] Wilson to Polk, March 15, 1920, Wilson Papers.
[12] Polk to Ambassador Wallace, March 15, 1920, *For. Rel., 1920* **2**: pp. 368-370. Polk objected to efforts to compel surrender of German-owned neutral securities, ostensibly to purchase raw materials necessary to meet reparations payments, and to interpretation of the Treaty of Peace to exclude previously seized German shipping and other property in computation of the initial reparations payment.

the area to suppress the Spartacists and restore order. The British representative at Berlin and the American commissioner reacted favorably, but the French delegate was evasive. France suggested permitting the entry of the force if Germany would consent to Allied occupation of Frankfurt as a guaranty of early withdrawal. Polk instructed Ambassador Wallace in Paris on March 22 to cooperate with his British colleague on the Council of Ambassadors in support of the German request, and he objected to the Frankfurt suggestion as an unnecessary extension of the occupation.[13] When Wallace voiced these views at the Council of Ambassadors, the French Foreign Minister replied that the United States might adopt a different attitude if it were in France's geographical situation of a common border with Germany.[14]

Colby reiterated American willingness to permit the police action in the Ruhr, while continuing to oppose any occupation of additional German territory. As he informed Wallace on April 2, the French scheme would result in "further irritating Germany perhaps even to [the] extent of bringing about common action between Communist forces in [the] Ruhr region and German governmental troops." [15] He restated the department's view to the American commissioner in Berlin, describing the Ebert government as "lamentably weak" but "the sole present alternative to a government of the extreme Right or the extreme Left." [16] Since the United States had not ratified the Treaty, Colby presented these views as an unofficial summary of the American attitude. When German troops entered the neutralized area, technically violating the peace

---

[13] *Ibid.* **2**: pp. 297-298.
[14] *Documents on British Foreign Policy, 1919-1939*, first series, edited by E. L. Woodward and R. Butler (16 v., London, 1947-1958) **9**: pp. 265-266.
[15] Colby to Wallace, March 24 and 26, and April 2, 1920, *For. Rel., 1920* **2**: pp. 298-299, 299-300, 302-303.
[16] *Ibid.* **2**: p. 308.

terms, the French government on April 6 promptly ordered its army to occupy Darmstadt and Frankfurt. Germany could only appeal to the League of Nations for a decision in the dispute.[17]

The American and British governments followed a parallel course in opposing French retaliation. When France protested the movement of German troops into the Ruhr, Colby advised Wilson that the United States should temporarily preserve silence until the situation was clarified. The President, however, viewed the French occupation of additional areas as "a very grave matter indeed," and he directed a probe of French intentions.[18] In the ensuing discussion with Ambassador Jusserand, Colby received assurances that France had no imperialistic ambitions and intended to keep its troops in the Frankfurt area only as long as German military forces remained in the Ruhr. The Secretary therefore agreed with Polk and other advisers that in view of the British and Italian objections to the French occupation a response from the United States could be postponed while awaiting further developments. Although he professed "no confidence whatever" in the French reassurances, seeing the French occupation as a final victory for the designs of Marshal Ferdinand Foch and others for a Rhine frontier, Wilson concurred, stating that he and Colby would discuss the entire problem soon.[19]

After the British and Italian governments expressed disapproval of the French occupation, Colby with the President's concurrence instructed Ambassador Wallace to communicate informally to the French Foreign Ministry the "deep concern" of the United States about the possible unfortunate consequences of the occupation of Frankfurt. Al-

---

[17] *Ibid.* **2**: pp. 311, 314.
[18] Colby to Wilson, April 6, 1920, Colby Papers; and Wilson to Colby, April 7, 1920, Wilson Papers.
[19] Colby to Wilson, April 7, 1920, Colby Papers; and Wilson to Colby, April 8, 1920, Wilson Papers. For the British position, see *Documents on British Foreign Policy* **7**: pp. 606-610, and **8**: pp. 220-223.

though the American government sympathized with French fears of German militarism, in its view the German government should be permitted to restore order in the Ruhr; any additional Allied occupation of German territory might "cause a junction of militaristic forces in Germany and elements . . . striving for revolution and overthrow of political and economic order." [20] According to an agreement made in August, 1919, and just then expiring, Germany had had the right to maintain some troops in the area; the United States hoped France would agree to renewal of the agreement, otherwise the removal of all German forces might trigger further disorders. The French government denied the need for larger German forces in the Ruhr and reiterated assurances that its troops would leave Frankfurt when the German army in excess of those permissable under the agreement withdrew from the Ruhr.[21] France replied to British complaints with a promise not to act again without consultation, but it did not recall its soldiers until May 17, 1920, after the Spartacist uprising had been suppressed and German troops were withdrawn.

In mid-April, the Allied premiers met at San Remo to discuss territorial questions and the assignment of Class A mandates. The Italian government wanted the United States to be represented, but Wilson was unwilling to permit more than an American observer at the conference. In his opinion, the British and French governments had departed so radically from the course established at the peace conference that the direction of their policies was incalculable. Ambassador Robert Underwood Johnson was in-

[20] Colby to Wilson, April 10, 1920, Colby Papers; and Colby to Wallace, April 12, 1920, *For. Rel., 1920* **2**: pp. 324-325.

[21] *Ibid.* **2**: pp. 325-326. The American government refused to permit its troops around Coblentz to be controlled by the Inter-Allied Rhineland Commission or to allow the area occupied by Americans to be utilized by France in military operations arising from the Ruhr incident (Colby to Wilson, April 8 and 10, 1920, Colby Papers; and *For. Rel., 1920* **2**: pp. 311-312).

structed to attend "solely as an observer and not as a participant." [22]

The Allies at San Remo requested the United States to assume a mandate for Armenia and, as a separate question, to arbitrate Armenia's border disputes with its neighbors.[23] Wilson was favorably inclined to accept the mandate when it should prove possible; earlier he had written his friend Cleveland H. Dodge that "I have set my heart on seeing this Government accept the mandate for Armenia." [24] Since Congress otherwise would be loath to assent, the President urged "legitimate propaganda" to develop public support for a mandate. He informed Colby that he would like to include Constantinople and had intended to recommend assumption of a mandate to Congress. Sir Auckland Geddes, the new British Ambassador, reported to London that Wilson and Colby were "extremely desirous" of forcing American acceptance of the mandate and had considered asking former Ambassador James W. Gerard to develop a plan for acting without the approval of Congress and had approached certain Republicans who were interested in the Middle East. Subsequently he supplied details of a plan for American aid to Armenia, short of the assumption of a mandate, and of Colby's inquiry whether the Allies were willing to reopen the question of control of Constantinople if the United States would assume its responsibility. The Foreign Secretary, Lord Curzon (Earl Curzon of Keddleston), noted on Geddes' dispatch that, while he considered reopening the Turkish Treaty unlikely, he would favor an American mandate for Armenia or the Caucasian republic: "I should witness with a grim delight their dealing with those States when in the hands of Soviet Governments." [25]

[22] Wilson to Colby, April 17, 1920, Wilson Papers; Colby to Wilson, April 20, 1920, Colby Papers; and *For. Rel., 1920* **1**: p. 2.
[23] Johnson to Colby, April 27, 1920, *For. Rel., 1920* **3**: pp. 779-783.
[24] Wilson to Dodge, April 19, 1920, Wilson Papers.
[25] *Documents on British Foreign Policy* **13**: pp. 70-72, 76.

In accordance with the President's instructions, Colby informed the Allies that Wilson agreed to act as arbitrator for Armenia, to do justice to those "poor people."[26] Colby wrote the President on May 20 that the Bolsheviks were threatening Armenia and that, since the Allies were unable to help, Wilson should urge Congress to approve a mandate lest the Armenian republic be wrecked and Bolshevism given an open road.[27] Because Congress was unwilling to accept a mandate—the Senate rebuffed Wilson on this subject, on June 1, 1920—nothing resulted from the first part of the Allied proposal.

Despite a British request, Wilson overruled the views of Colby, Polk, and Davis, and decided not to have the United States represented even unofficially at the conference called at Spa in early July between the Supreme Council and German representatives to arrange and apportion reparations from Germany.[28] The United States had not ratified the Versailles Treaty; in addition, there was some resentment that Great Britain had broken off conversation with the Treasury Department on repayment of war loans to the United States.

The Teschen boundary dispute between Czechoslovakia and Poland, involving riots and the imposition of martial law, revealed Wilson's mounting resentment of the Anglo-French role as the arbiters of postwar Europe. Although the United States had not been represented on several boundary commissions, because of its failure to ratify the Versailles Treaty, Wilson insisted that an American must

---

[26] Wilson to Colby, May 11, 1920, Wilson Papers; Colby to Wallace, May 17, 1920, *For. Rel., 1920* **3**: p. 783. Wilson's arbitral ruling was transmitted to the Supreme Council on November 24, 1920, *ibid.* **3**: pp. 789-804.
[27] Colby Papers.
[28] Colby to Wilson, May 27, and Wilson to Colby, May 29, 1920, Wilson Papers; June 8, 1920, Daniels Diary; and *For. Rel., 1920* **2**: p. 393. The United States was unofficially represented throughout this period at the work of the Reparations Commission. An unofficial delegate was also sent to the League-called International Financial Conference.

be included in the body established to arbitrate or to hold a plebiscite in the Duchy of Teschen.[29] Then in July the Supreme Council, meeting at Spa, decided to resolve the problem itself. With the concurrence of the two interested states, the council drew a boundary line in the disputed area. The British, aware that Washington refused to recognize the decisions of a council on which it was not represented, were anxious for American cooperation.[30] Colby advised Wilson that, since Poland and Czechoslovakia had agreed to disposition by the Supreme Council, and the United States had no immediate interest in the problem, he saw no reason why Ambassador Wallace should not indicate the government's acquiescence to the Council of Ambassadors.[31] Ambassador Geddes subsequently explained that because Poland insisted upon arbitration and the Czechs wanted a plebiscite, the two states had intimated that they gladly would accept a solution by the Supreme Council, which had now complied with a decision that it was certain the United States would support in the interests of peace. Apparently at Wilson's direction, however, Colby instructed Wallace that such questions properly should be submitted to arbitration, "and not [resolved] by imposing boundaries upon weaker powers by the principal powers."[32] He thought that Poland and Czechoslovakia had assented only with reluctance to the solution by the great powers, but because of the gravity of the situation in Teschen the United States was willing to

[29] *For. Rel., 1920* **2**: pp. 38-39.
[30] *Documents on British Foreign Policy* **8**: pp. 548-551, 556-557.
[31] Colby to Wilson, July 16, 1920, Colby Papers. When the League Council appointed three jurists to render an advisory opinion on the Swedish-Finnish conflict over possession of the Aaland Islands, Colby suggested that Elihu Root should serve on the commission. Wilson responded negatively: "I have absolutely no faith in Mr. Elihu Root and feel sure that he would do something to prove his falseness if we delegated him." Abram I. Elkus finally was selected (Colby to Wilson, July 18, and Wilson to Colby, July 20, 1920, Wilson Papers; and *For. Rel., 1920* **1**: p. 35).
[32] Geddes to Colby, and Colby to Wallace, July 21, 1920, *For. Rel., 1920* **1**: pp. 46-47, 50-52.

accept the line temporarily until it could be submitted to an impartial commission for rectification.

Privately, Colby informed Geddes that President Wilson was adamant that the express and unreserved consent of the Polish and Czech governments to a solution by the Supreme Council must be obtained before the United States could acquiesce; otherwise Wilson would view the affair as a "departure from self determination" contrary to the principles upon which the peace of Europe was to be reestablished. Lord Curzon was greatly distressed at Washington's failure to understand that the disputants wanted the issue settled with the least possible delay: "I shall really despair if the Americans, by again reverting to their tactics of delays and hesitation, once more succeed in frustrating settlement. . . ."[33] In another statement to Geddes, Colby reiterated the President's view that Poland and Czechoslovakia had agreed to accept a decision by the Supreme Council "only with great reluctance," a view that the Earl of Derby, the British Ambassador in Paris, attributed to a misleading French language version of the decision at Spa.[34]

Ambassador Wallace reported from Paris that perhaps he had failed to emphasize the unqualified readiness of Poland and Czechoslovakia to accept a solution by the Supreme Council; the British and the French governments, however, were willing to concur in the proposed commission, but only if it confined its task to local adjustments in the boundary drawn by the council.[35] It was obvious that Wallace considered the Allied policy the wiser one and feared unnecessary delay if the United States insisted on a complete reexamination of the decision. Nevertheless, instructions sent over Colby's name, on July 26, replied that

[33] Geddes to Curzon, July 22, and Curzon to the British Ambassador in Paris, July 23, 1920, *Documents on British Foreign Policy* **10**: pp. 709, 710-711.
[34] Colby to Geddes, July 23, 1920, *For. Rel., 1920* **1**: pp. 53-55; and *Documents on British Foreign Policy* **10**: pp. 711-712.
[35] Wallace to Colby, July 23, 1920, *For. Rel., 1920* **1**: pp. 55-57, 57-59.

the department's position was not based primarily upon an impression of the reluctant attitudes of Poland and Czechoslovakia, but upon principle and correct procedure. The instruction complained of "the arbitrary decision" of the Supreme Council at Spa, settling the issue without consulting the United States and merely notifying it after the fact with the express assumption that it would acquiesce: "we do not recognize the propriety of such disposition being made without consulting or obtaining our approval. . . ."[36] Yet Wallace's recommendation was approved that the United States accept the solution adopted by the Supreme Council, with the Council of Ambassadors, including the American Ambassador, to be entrusted to make such local changes and adjustments in the boundary as was deemed advisable.

The British were greatly agitated when Wallace communicated the essence of his latest instructions to the Council of Ambassadors. Lord Curzon pointed out to Wallace that the American government was operating on the mistaken assumption that Poland and Czechoslovakia had received an imposed settlement.[37] The American reply, he lamented, showed a "complete failure to understand the actual situation. . . ."[38] Geddes promptly protested to Colby, who seemed "dumbfounded" at the instructions sent over his name on July 26. The British envoy could only explain the incident as done without the Secretary's knowledge by Hugh Gibson, the Minister to Poland who was temporarily in Washington; Gibson's motive, he speculated, was to embarrass the French.[39] In all probability,

---

[36] Colby to Wallace, July 26, 1920, *ibid.* 1: pp. 59-60.
[37] Curzon to Geddes, July 26, 1920, F.O.115/2632/Teschen 1 (9), British Foreign Office Correspondence, Public Record Office, London (hereafter cited as F.O.).
[38] Curzon to Geddes, July 27, 1920, F.O.115/2632/Teschen 1 (10).
[39] Geddes to Curzon, July 28, 1920, *Documents on British Foreign Policy* 10: pp. 713-714.

however, Gibson had acted with Colby's permission though perhaps he erred on the side of too harsh a tone.

After Colby had tried to assuage British irritation, Wallace's arrangement was approved by the Council of Ambassadors on July 28. Wallace, however, was directed by Colby not to sign his own agreement. Despite the Ambassador's opinion that he should be permitted to sign, Colby persisted in refusal:

> The Department feels that there has not been a willingness on the part of the Allies to consider this Government's impartial and disinterested opinion of this question and that there has been a persistent tendency to try to carry through a settlement of it without due regard for this Government's views.[40]

Yet Colby insisted that an American must serve on the commission, which Wallace viewed as diplomatically questionable if he were not permitted to sign. The final result was that the United States was represented by an unofficial delegate, who was withdrawn in early March, 1921.[41]

The Teschen affair graphically illustrated the deterioration of American relations with the Allies in Europe. Geddes probably divined correctly that Colby was not entirely in sympathy with official policy on the issue. But the sharp tone of the exchanges was not just the work of a subordinate such as Minister Gibson. Instead it reflected the distrust with which President Wilson now viewed the major Allied powers and his bitterness at actions which he regarded as undermining a just peace.

3.

President Wilson foresaw severe commercial competition with Great Britain in the postwar years. In March, 1920, he wrote to Polk that such a struggle seemed imminent, and that he was afraid that Great Britain would prove

[40] *For. Rel., 1920* **1**: pp. 67, 69-70.
[41] *Ibid.* **1**: pp. 70-73.

"capable of as great commercial savagery as Germany."[42] Previously, in August, 1919, Lansing had protested sharply against an Anglo-Persian Treaty, which he charged had been negotiated in secrecy and seriously impaired the sovereignty of Persia.[43] The Standard Oil Company of New York complained to the State Department that its activities in Palestine were being interfered with by the British authorities. The war had demonstrated the importance of oil for military and economic purposes, and there was increasing concern in the United States about supposedly inadequate domestic reserves, in contrast to Britain's alleged plans to monopolize the world's petroleum resources. Lansing instructed Ambassador John W. Davis in London to intimate that the American government expected equal privileges for its citizens with British and other nationals in exploiting the resources of Mesopotamia and Palestine.[44] Early in 1920 Davis was again requested to remind the British government that its restrictive oil policies barring new exploitations or explorations were arousing criticism in the United States, and to reiterate America's vital concern in retaining oil concessions obtained during the period of Turkish rule.[45]

The State Department strongly protested any attempt to exclude the United States from negotiations establishing League mandates in the Middle East. At the Allied con-

[42] Wilson to Polk, March 4, 1920, Wilson Papers. The President objected to the new British Ambassador, Sir Auckland Geddes, because he allegedly closely represented British commercial interests; Wilson preferred a more purely political figure.

[43] *For. Rel., 1919* **2**: pp. 698-717. The British government claimed that it had informed Colonel House of its intentions. The treaty granted Great Britain the right to provide military officers and equipment to modernize the Persian army, to advance loans, and the encouragement of railroad development. The Persian Majlis refused to approve the agreement.

[44] Lansing to Davis, October 30, 1919, *ibid.* **2**: pp. 259-260. See John A. DeNovo, "The Movement for an Aggressive American Oil Policy Abroad, 1918-1920," *Amer. Hist. Rev.* **61** (1956): pp. 854-876.

[45] Lansing to Davis, February 4, and Polk to the Chargé in London, March 17, 1920, *For. Rel., 1920* **2**: pp. 649-650, 650-651.

ference at San Remo, in April, 1920, an Anglo-French agreement was concluded relating to Mesopotamia and Palestine, and subsequently published, that appeared to give French citizens preferential treatment in the exploitation of oil in the projected British mandate in Mesopotamia. Aware of the bad press that the announcement of the agreement probably would receive in the United States, the Foreign Office drafted an explanation to Ambassador Geddes denying that any exclusive exploitation rights had been reserved for Britain or France; all that had occurred was that France, lacking a supply of its own and greatly in need of fuel during the reconstruction of its war-ravaged economy, had been guaranteed a supply of 25 per cent of the output at ordinary commercial prices.[46] Colby directed Ambassador Davis to point out to the British Foreign Office that the arrangement seemed to be inconsistent with the principle of equality of treatment that had been accepted at the Paris Peace Conference.[47] The Allies were in the process of imposing the Treaty of Sèvres upon defeated Turkey.

For some months Geddes had been reporting on the ill-feeling against the British being worked up by the oil interests in the United States. Standard Oil especially was seen as the chief villain in the propaganda campaign. Curzon apparently was outraged at these tactics, writing Geddes that the United States already controlled over 80 per cent of the world's known oil supply and yet wanted to block all others.[48] Consequently, on August 9, the British Foreign Office responded to Colby's protest in a very sharp note, almost sarcastic in tone, denying any intention of challenging the alleged supremacy of American oil inter-

[46] F.O.371/5085/E8622/20/44.
[47] Colby to Davis, July 26, 1920. *For. Rel., 1920* **2**: pp. 658-659.
[48] *Documents on British Foreign Policy* **13**: pp. 66, 256-257, 273-274. The Foreign Office had intercepted a letter by an American named Gallacher, apparently a Standard Oil employee in the Middle East, that seemed to corroborate Standard's leading role in the anti-British campaign (F.O.37/5085/E7604/20/44).

ests, and declaring that a British or French monopoly was not sought in Mesopotamia, where other interests would not be excluded. According to Lord Curzon's note, the draft arrangements for the mandates in Mesopotamia and Palestine would secure economic equality of opportunity for the nationals of League members and would be submitted to the League Council for approval. The Foreign Secretary expressed appreciation of American suggestions for discussing the terms of the mandates, but stated that could "only properly be discussed at the Council of the League of Nations by the signatories of the Covenant." [49]

After a long delay, occasioned by the elections in the United States, Colby in November secured Wilson's approval of a very smoothly phrased reply to the British note.[50] Curzon was reminded that the United States, because of its role in the war, could not be excluded from the equality of treatment to be accorded all League members, nor could it be denied a voice in the framing of the terms of the mandate agreements. Colby requested, therefore, that the United States be given copies of the mandate drafts for its consideration prior to League action. He pointed out to Curzon the widespread interest in the resources of Mesopotamia, "a potential subject of economic strife," and he recalled to the British Foreign Secretary that the mandate system had been devised primarily to eliminate international conflicts and rivalries for the exclusive control of the resources and markets of colonial and dependent territories.[51] Moreover, Colby denied that the United States dominated the world's oil reserves or that the concern of the American government was dictated by economic considerations. Colby thereby re-iterated the Wilsonian faith in an open-door world as essential not only

[49] *For. Rel., 1920* **2**: pp. 663-667.
[50] Colby to Wilson, November 19, 1920, Colby Papers.
[51] Colby to Davis, November 23, 1920, *For. Rel., 1920* **2**: pp. 669-673.

to America's prosperity but world peace. As Wilson had described it, Colby's note was an admirable one. Later, with the President's concurrence, Colby notified the British, French, and Italian governments that America insisted upon equality of treatment within any spheres of influence established in Anatolia.[52] At the same tiime he branded as preposterous reports in the London press that Anglo-American tensions were leading toward war.[53]

Although the British Foreign Office did not reply to Colby's note of November 23 until after the Wilson administration had left office, exploratory discussions were held earlier. One complicating factor was that France seemed to want to withdraw from the San Remo agreement, and until that had been resolved the British government was unsure of "exactly what policy is to be followed about oil in Mesopotamia."[54] On February 24, 1921, Colby and Davis met with Geddes to discuss the controversy and Britain's contemplated formal reply to the American demands.[55] Geddes acknowledged that the American government was entitled to a voice in framing the mandate agreements, but he excused the Allied failure to do so on the grounds that the United States had chosen not to be represented on the Supreme Council where the decisions were made. Colby refused to accept the excuse and reiterated the State Department's position that it must be consulted on all such problems through regular diplomatic channels. Ultimately, the Allies were to comply during the twenties with the American demands for a voice in these mandates and for the admission of American oil firms into the Middle East petroleum fields.

[52] Colby to Wilson, November 27, 1920, Colby Papers. See Carl P. Parrini, *Heir to Empire: United States Economic Diplomacy* (Pittsburgh, 1969), pp. 139-147.
[53] February 9, 1921, New York *Times*.
[54] F.O.371/5638/A45, 495, and 745/44/45; and 371/6360/E2027/382/93.
[55] State Department File 462.00R29/3511, Foreign Affairs Division, National Archives. Hereafter cited as S. D., followed by the document number.

President Wilson was increasingly hostile toward America's associates in the recent Great War. Even before his illness in the fall of 1919, he had expressed great distress at reports from Paris about the continuing scramble for territorial gain by the victorious Allies. He commented to Lansing on one occasion, specifically about Roumania but having a more general application: "When I see such conduct as this . . . and when I think of the greed and utter selfishness of it all, I am almost inclined to refuse to permit this country to be a member of the League of Nations when it is composed of such intriguers and robbers. I am disposed to throw up the whole business and get out." [56] Subsequently he often complained to Colby of "the ugly disposition towards the United States of the four Powers now attempting to run the affairs of the world. . . ." [57] When Colby transmitted the suggestion of the American Minister in Switzerland that he be permitted to attend the convening of the League Assembly as an observer, Wilson declined: there would be no great advantage in being represented at such councils where the "other great Powers are now mismanaging the world. . . ." [58]

One of Wilson's most determined efforts at the Paris Peace Conference in 1919 had been waged against Italy's desire for the port city of Fiume and additional territory along the Adriatic coast. In his view, justice required that Fiume should be part of the new Yugoslav state, or else connected to her as a free city under the League of Nations. The issue had not been settled and subsequently the British and French governments were inclined to arrange a compromise that Wilson deemed unwise and a betrayal of principle. When the British and French premiers supported a "compromise" placing Fiume under Italian sov-

[56] Entry of August 20, 1919, Confidential Memoranda, Lansing Papers.
[57] Wilson to Colby, November 9, 1920, Wilson Papers.
[58] Colby to Wilson, November 11, and Wilson to Colby, November 12, 1920, ibid.

ereignty with some alleged territorial concessions to Yugoslavia along the Adriatic coast, the President had the State Department dispatch a very vigorous note on February 9, 1920. The Allies were sharply warned that, if they persisted, President Wilson would seriously consider withdrawing the Versailles Treaty from the Senate and the abandonment of the settlement of remaining problems of the peace. The proposed disposition of Fiume was contrary to the principles for which America had entered the war and would raise the question if the United States could "on any terms cooperate with its European associates in the great work of maintaining the peace of the world. . . ." The President would have to "take under serious consideration the withdrawal of the treaty with Germany" from the Senate, and the leaving of the problem of the determination and enforcement of peace terms to the Allies.[59]

A furor ensued in Europe at this apparent ultimatum. The British Prime Minister, David Lloyd George, remarked at an Allied conference in London that it was very difficult to know how to address Wilson "whose psychological condition was so uncertain." [60] French diplomatic circles complained bitterly that America refused to participate in the work of the Supreme Council and yet demanded that the premiers must shape decisions in accordance with America's wishes. That reaction, and the encouragement the warning gave to critics of the Treaty in America, who used the incident to claim that America should never have become involved in Europe, caused a White House spokesman to narrow Wilson's threat of withdrawal to the Adriatic area only. London and Paris, in conciliatory replies, then denied any intention of ignoring

---

[59] S.D.File 763.72119/8833, 9267, 9284, Archives; *British and Foreign State Papers, 1914-1920* (London, 1918-1923) **113**: pp. 842-846; and February 16 and 17, 1920, New York *Times*.

[60] Allied Conference in London, February 16, 1920, *Documents on British Foreign Policy* **7**: p. 75.

the United States and in effect complained of the lack of American representation when these questions came up. Wilson's following notes were also less rigid and indicated a willingness to accept a freely made Italian-Yugoslav arrangement, which the Allies welcomed.[61]

Yet the President still was greatly distressed by the Treaty of Rapallo, concluded on November 12, 1920, between Italy and Yugoslavia, that settled the Fiume dispute on the basis of an independent or free city and gave Italy Zara and a number of Dalmatian islands. As he wrote Colby, "Italy has absolutely no bowels and is evidently planning a new Alsace-Lorraine on the other side of the Adriatic which is sure to contain the seeds of another European war." If that happened, he hoped Italy would "get the stuffing licked out of her." [62] On the same day as this letter, he also wrote Colby of his objections to following the Allied example of resuming diplomatic relations with Bulgaria: "I have found the Bulgarians the most avaricious and brutal of the smaller nations that had to be dealt with in the war . . . though for a long time my vote was for Roumania in those respects. Being no longer committed to Roumania, I can perhaps transfer my suffrages to Bulgaria." [63]

Deprived of a significant voice in these post-Versailles peace arrangements, both by the Senate's failure to approve the Treaty and by his own choice, the embittered and disillusioned President at times seemed almost ready to wash his hands of European affairs and to welcome an American return to its prewar traditional pattern of non-involvement. He declined to let the United States be represented at the forthcoming Brussels conference on the reparations to be assessed against Germany, and the American Ambassador to France was instructed to give notice of his withdrawal

---

[61] *Ibid.* **7**: pp. 76-80, 250-253; and S.D.File 763.72119/9267, 9284, Archives.
[62] Wilson to Colby, November 15, 1920, Wilson Papers.
[63] Wilson to Colby, November 15, 1920, *ibid.*

from the Council of Ambassadors.[64] As Norman Davis then informed Wallace, Wilson also deemed it advisable to withdraw the American observer from the Reparations Commission for, apart from Republican intentions, the Allies showed an increasing tendency to ignore American views, as in regard to mandates, and "only consult . . . in cases where they look to us for assistance." [65]

When Davis inquired whether Congress should be asked for permission for the United States to join an International Road Congress, Wilson replied negatively, because "I think it is inadvisable at this time to seek any permanent association with the European nations in view of the uncertainty of the basis upon which all such relations will rest in the future. . . ." [66] Since there were strong indications that the incoming Harding administration planned a separate peace treaty with Germany, Colby advised Wilson not to lodge a *caveat* or protest against the reparations settlement then being concluded by the Allied Powers.[67]

It was an ironic terminal note for an administration that had sought to lead America into new paths of world responsibilities and leadership. Admittedly, events in the Senate and the outcome of the 1920 elections greatly impaired the influence of the Wilson administration abroad. Yet from the fall of 1919 on, before the rejection of the Versailles Treaty was certain, it would appear that President Wilson and his advisers in the State Department at times curtailed America's role in Europe more than was necessary. The motives were not merely ones of political strategy and necessity, but included Wilson's bitter personal reaction to the checks administered in the Senate, increasing resentment and suspicions of French and British purposes that probably were not wholly justified and that obviously

[64] Wilson to Davis, December 9, 1920, *ibid.;* and *For. Rel., 1921* 1: pp. 3-4.
[65] *For. Rel., 1921* 1: pp. 5-6.
[66] Wilson to Davis, January 10, 1921, Wilson Papers.
[67] Colby to Wilson, February 4, 1921, *ibid.*

failed to give due weight to France's security fears, and a growing administration sense of disillusionment with the Great Crusade in Europe and its aftermath. Of course, much of the business before the peacemakers in 1920 concerned the United States only peripherally. Issues of mandates, reparations, and postwar European financial affairs, however, were of more direct interest, but the American policy of unofficial observers or non-representation at various Allied conferences and League-sponsored meetings made it difficult if not impossible to exert meaningful influence on the handling of these problems. If a more consistent policy of involvement had been followed, within the range of current political possibilities in America, it might have been possible to have exerted a greater ameliorating influence on a number of the postwar issues. Moreover, such involvement might have carried over into the Harding era to a greater degree than was to happen. Instead, Wilson was pointing the way toward the Republican course of limited internationalism.

4.

Colby's most significant leadership in European affairs was in the area of Russian policy. Even so, of course, the essential ingredients of his policy had emerged before he took office, during the Lansing era.

As in 1918, it was American policy toward the several movements for independence within parts of the former Russian empire to withhold formal recognition until the Russian people should achieve a unified government of their own to resolve such problems. The former Baltic provinces which had declared their independence as the new states of Lithuania, Latvia, and Estonia, were not recognized although their existence was apparently regarded with some sympathy by the State Department. Lansing instructed the

American commissioner at Riga, in regard to peace talks between the Baltic states and the government of Soviet Russia, to communicate informally to the Latvian authorities the American skepticism about compromise attempts: "The experience of this Government has convinced it that it is not practicable for non-Bolshevik governments to deal with the Bolshevists," for the "ultimate purpose of the latter is to overturn all non-Bolshevik governments and seeming compromises which they may make with these are presumably but temporary and tactical expedients." [68] The American government kept its role informal, however, to avoid implying an obligation to aid Latvia and the other Baltic states if peace were not concluded with the Soviet regime.[69]

A similar attitude was taken toward Poland. When the American Minister at Warsaw inquired whether the Department wished the Polish government to resist a Soviet invasion of the areas claimed by Poland east of the ethnic line (the so-called Curzon Line) laid down by the Supreme Council at the Paris Peace Conference in December 1919 or to make peace, Lansing replied on February 7, 1920, that the United States was not in a position to assume any responsibility for advising Poland in the matter. The Minister was told for his own information, however, that Lansing thought it would be most unfortunate if Poland interpreted American silence to imply that any military and economic assistance would be forthcoming if armistice proposals by Soviet Russia were rejected.[70] Colby reiterated Lansing's policy, when shortly after he took office he refused to become involved in Finnish-Soviet relations.[71]

[68] Lansing to Polk at Paris, for the Commissioner at Riga, November 21, 1919, *Papers Relating to the Foreign Relations of the United States, Russia, 1919* (Washington, 1937), pp. 742-743.
[69] *Ibid.*, p. 747; and *For. Rel., 1920* **3**: pp. 642-643, 646. See Albert N. Tarulis, *American-Baltic Relations, 1918-1922* (Washington, 1965).
[70] *For. Rel., 1920* **3**: pp. 377, 378.
[71] S.D.File 861.00/6608, Archives.

Although the American government continued to refuse to recognize the Soviet regime in Russia, it was under increasing pressure to remove trade restrictions applying to the Bolshevik-controlled areas. On February 25 a Soviet proposal for negotiations on recognition was transmitted to the department by the American Minister in Sweden; the Bolshevik regime disavowed any purpose of interfering in the internal affairs of the United States and professed to desire only peace and trade.[72] The trade question became acute when Prime Minister Lloyd George told Parliament that force having failed to restore Russia to sanity, trade seemed to be the most promising—and of course profitable—approach. Interim Secretary Polk informed Ambassador Wallace at Paris that the Department was prepared to discuss with the Allies common measures to remove trade restrictions and he inquired whether Britain and France had any plans to prevent the Bolshevik regime from disposing abroad illegally obtained securities and valuables when commerce should be resumed. Citizens should be warned that conditions were uncertain in Russia and that only limited protection could be given to their activities in areas under Bolshevik control. Polk's instructions made clear that the United States was not prepared to recognize Soviet Russia nor to permit its agents on American soil: "The American Government, however, has not received substantial evidence that the good faith of the Soviet regime has been sufficiently established or its character so altered . . . as to justify an effort to renew even the informal relations that were in being until August 1918."[73] Hence the United States was not to participate in the trade talks scheduled by the Allies with Soviet representatives in London.

After Colby took office, the State Department suggested

[72] *For. Rel., 1920* **3**: p. 447.
[73] Polk to Wallace, March 6, 1920, *ibid.* **3**: pp. 703-704.

April 10 as the date to lift trade restrictions. Britain and France postponed action, however, pending the outcome of the London talks with a Soviet trade delegation led by L. B. Krassin, the Soviet Commissar for Trade and Industry. The British government was apprehensive that premature action by the United States would hamper a satisfactory solution.[74] When the issue was discussed at a Cabinet meeting on May 4, President Wilson expressed distrust of the Allied governments. He thought that to open commercial relations with Soviet Russia would soon involve its diplomatic recognition. Colby and Joshua W. Alexander, Secretary of Commerce, believed that it might be possible to trade without extending recognition; Alexander noted that American business groups feared that England was controlling trade with Russia while the United States neglected its opportunities.[75] There also was agitation within the American Federation of Labor for the reopening of trade. In reply to a telegram from Samuel Gompers, Colby tried to head off embarrassing demands. His message was read at the A. F. of L. convention, and after heated debate a resolution advocating recognition of the Soviets or the raising of trade restrictions was blocked. Colby's telegram pointed out that at several conferences held in Europe on the restoration of trade the Soviet government had demanded recognition as necessary to renew commerce:

While this Government has no desire to interfere with the internal affairs of the Russian people or to suggest the kind of government that they should have, the existing regime in Russia does not represent the will or consent of any considerable proportion of the Russian people. It repudiates every principle of harmonious and trustful relations . . . and is based upon the negation of honor and good faith. . . .[76]

[74] *Ibid.* **3**: pp. 708, 709-711.
[75] May 4, 1920, Daniels Diary.
[76] Colby to Wilson, June 11, 1920, Colby Papers; and June 16, 1920, New York *Times*.

The Krassin trade mission to London aroused deep concern in Washington. In discussing British intentions with Ambassador Geddes, in late May, Colby voiced his doubts about trade and negotiations of any kind with the Soviets:

> The Secretary of State told me that his policy was to keep clear of Russia until the Soviet power collapsed and that he felt that for America even to attempt to trade with Russia would not be wise. He said that in his opinion, based upon the best reports from Russia that the State Department was able to obtain, it seemed probable that the end of the Soviet power was rapidly approaching. He believed that even July, more probably August, might see the collapse of that power.[77]

On June 19, the Ambassador cabled the Foreign Office again about Washington's anxiety: "There is no doubt American Government is seriously disturbed . . . and believes that full recognition of Soviet Government is contemplated."[78] Colby, he reported, raised the issue at least once every week, and the President was "deeply interested." It seems clear that while Colby was persuaded that trade restrictions must be lifted, like the President he had little enthusiasm for that step and was determined not to permit it to open the way toward any form of diplomatic recognition. The great Red Scare in the United States may have been ebbing as May Day passed without a predicted Bolshevik uprising in America, but Colby's hostility to communism had not abated. Colby told Geddes that the United States might follow the British course on trade if convinced it was sound, but he was very fearful that reopening channels of commerce might strengthen the Bolshevik war machine.[79]

Lord Curzon tried to reassure the Americans. As he instructed Geddes, there was no question of making peace with the Soviet government or recognizing it.[80] The United

[77] Geddes to Curzon, May 31, 1920, F.O.115/2628/Russia 12 (2).
[78] F.O.115/2628/Russia 12 (5).
[79] Geddes to Curzon, June 20, 1919, *Documents on British Foreign Policy* **12**: pp. 739-740.
[80] Curzon to Geddes, June 24, 1919, *ibid.* **12**: pp. 742-743.

States had been invited to participate in the London trade talks that developed out of an earlier decision by the Supreme Council of which the State Department was aware. Resumption of trade now would make Russian supplies of grain and raw materials available to a needy Europe and, in Curzon's view, probably would lead to the downfall of the Red regime. In any case, not even talks about trade would be continued unless the Soviets would promise to release all British prisoners and to cease revolutionary activity in the Middle East and the Caucasus. Perhaps the American government was reassured by these answers. Probably more reassuring, however, were obvious signs of a growing French disinterest in the trade talks and the disruptions caused by the Russo-Polish War. Not until March, 1921, was the Anglo-Soviet Trade Agreement to be signed.[81]

During Colby's absence at the Democratic Convention, Undersecretary Davis obtained Wilson's approval for a public statement that although trade restrictions were being removed, there was to be no change in recognition policy and no official support could be given to those citizens engaging in commerce with Russia.[82] The removal of restrictions was announced on July 7. Commerce could be resumed except in war materials, but travel and mail restrictions were to be continued.[83] The lure of trade, which finally was to facilitate recognition in 1933, was obviously too strong to be completely resisted.

The Russo-Polish War, from April to October, 1920, resulted in a reiteration of American policy against dismemberment of Russia and a clear and vigorous statement of the

---

[81] See George F. Kennan, *Russia and the West under Lenin and Stalin* (Boston, 1960), pp. 172-175.

[82] Davis to Wilson, June 23, 1920, Wilson Papers; Davis to Colby, June 25, 1920, The Papers of Norman H. Davis (Library of Congress, Manuscripts Division); and Wilson to Colby, July 3, 1920, Wilson Papers.

[83] *For. Rel., 1920* **3**: pp. 171, 715-717. The Federal Reserve System would not accept Soviet gold.

reasons for non-recognition of the Soviet government.[84] At first successful, by June the Polish forces had suffered serious reverses at the hands of the Red Army, while the Soviet government showed little interest in armistice terms suggested by the Allies. When it was proposed that any Polish-Bolshevik armistice negotiations should be broadened into a general conference to recognize the Soviet government and solve the Russian problem, presumably on the basis of partition, Colby expressed America's opposition. The United States government desired the integrity of Poland preserved and therefore sympathized with arrangements for a Polish-Soviet armistice, but it was unable to perceive how recognition of the Bolshevik regime could promote a peaceful solution to the problems of Europe: "For that reason the Department is opposed to any relations with the Bolshevik Government in excess of the narrowest limits within which the arranging of an armistice can be kept." [85] Colby pointed out that the American government, as it had made clear on July 8,[86] had consistently declined to deal with the Bolsheviks, because any negotiations would incur "a sacrifice of moral strength" in return for illusory material advantages. Since the department also believed that dismemberment of Russia would only delay or complicate the achievement of a lasting solution, it had refused to recognize the independence of the Baltic states.

[84] Colby informally urged the unrecognized Lithuanian government to settle peacefully the Vilna dispute with Poland, and warned that any Lithuanian military cooperation with the Bolsheviks would create a most unfavorable impression (*ibid.* **3**: pp. 650-651). He also wrote the President that he agreed with the suggestion of Minister Gibson (to Poland) that a message from Wilson would steady the critical situation in that country. Wilson replied that, despite his deep sympathy with Poland, ". . . I think the time has passed when personal intervention on my part . . . with regard to foreign politics would be of service . . ." (Colby to Wilson, July 18, and Wilson to Colby, July 20, 1920, Colby Papers).

[85] Colby to Ambassador Davis and other representatives abroad, August 2, 1920, *For. Rel., 1920* **3**: pp. 461-463.

[86] *Ibid.* **3**: p. 717.

Colby fully shared the views of his predecessor, Lansing, that any kind of relations with the Bolshevik government was undesirable. Apparently he felt even more deeply than had Lansing about the allegedly immoral nature of the Communist regime and movement. According to one historian, a friend of Raymond Robins called on the Secretary and reported that for nearly two hours Colby had "denounced Russia with a wealth of expression. . . ."[87]

Colby's strongly anti-Soviet views in part reflected the influence of John Spargo of Vermont. The author of a number of books on Socialism and Bolshevism, Spargo later was to be selected by historian Samuel Flagg Bemis to write a brief sketch of Colby for Bemis' series on American secretaries of state. Spargo was one of the small number of prewar Socialist leaders who had supported America's entry into the war. He viewed Russia as vital to the war-expanded American economy, and feared Japanese and German efforts at economic and political domination of that war-ravaged country. He expressed his views to an appreciative Lansing in late 1919, and subsequently wrote directly to President Wilson.[88] After Colby's appointment, Spargo sent his congratulations and called attention to his recent book, *Russia as an American Problem*, the product he claimed of twenty-five years of study.[89]

The volume deplored the Balkanization of Russia through the emergence of a number of independent petty states in the Baltic and other areas, which would deprive Russia of access to the sea. A wiser solution would be local autonomy within a federated state. America had a great stake in the future of Russia because a healthy world was incompatible

---

[87] William A. Williams, *American-Russian Relations, 1781-1947* (New York, 1952), p. 174.

[88] Spargo to Wilson, March 19, 1920, S.D.File 861.00/6610, Archives.

[89] Spargo to Colby, February 26, 1920, Colby Papers. He sent a similar letter to Wilson. Ronald Radosh, "John Spargo and Wilson's Russian Policy, 1920," *Jour. Amer. Hist.* **52** (1965): pp. 548-565, examines Spargo's influence on American policy makers.

with an anarchic Russia. Humanitarian, political, and economic considerations made Russia of vital importance to the postwar international order.[90] In a postscript to the book, dated January, 1920, Spargo attributed the collapse of the Kolchak regime in Siberia and that of other anti-Bolshevik movements to blunderings by the Allied and Associated Powers, their failure to adopt a clear policy of material and moral support. Bolshevism was "militarism gone mad." The regime, therefore, should not be recognized: "It is to be hoped that the honor of America will not be sullied by any such action. The crimes of the Bolsheviki against civilization . . . have been too monstrous and too systematically contrived and pursued to warrant our having any relations with them." Recent moderately phrased overtures from Lenin and his lieutenants could not be accepted at face value, for they were merely tactical devices based on "the perverted philosophy" that truth and honor were "bourgeois conceptions," while "treachery and deceit are legitimate [Soviet] weapons." Spargo concluded, "It is of the essence of the faith of the whole movement that to make agreements without the least intention of keeping them is a valuable proletarian method of class warfare."[91] Until the Bolshevik government changed for the better, the United States should withhold recognition while giving material support to any anti-Bolshevik movements in Russia. If the regime did not collapse, however, trade would probably soon have to be resumed, but he thought that could be done through the Russian cooperatives without recognizing the Soviet government. A general war against the Bolsheviks would have the unfortunate consequences of strengthening their popular appeal in Russia, and the United States should have no part in dismembering that country by complying with the plans of Roumanian or Polish imperialists.

[90] John Spargo, *Russia as an American Problem* (New York & London, 1920), pp. 1-11.
[91] *Ibid.*, pp. 337-344.

America instead should make a great effort to secure a large share of the Russian market, not for exploitative purposes but to help promote the emergence of a strong and free Russia.[92]

Colby read excerpts from Spargo's volume and, greatly impressed, he consulted him as an expert on socialism and Russia.[93] In a letter to Colby on July 31, repeated in a subsequent exchange, Spargo recommended release of a general statement on the American policy of non-recognition toward Soviet Russia, a statement that would urge other nations to cooperate in treating that regime as an "outlaw nation."[94] Spargo's ideas were to be incorporated in the note to Italy on August 10.

The note of August 10 was occasioned by alarm at the advance of Soviet armies against the Polish forces. The Secretary of the Italian Embassy called on Undersecretary Davis, on August 5, and expressed the view that the United States could exert great moral influence to help resolve the Polish-Soviet controversy if it would participate in a proposed conference or issue a general statement of policy. Davis replied that the American government had not yet decided to take any action, but that "we have little or no confidence in the wisdom of negotiating with the Bolsheviks or the possibility of making any agreements with them which can be depended upon."[95] Yet conditions in Poland were desperate and that country seemed on the verge of collapse unless outside aid could be obtained. Because the

[92] *Ibid.*, pp. 344-348.
[93] At the Cabinet meeting on August 3, Colby proposed that Spargo write a statement for release on the dangers of Bolshevik propaganda; Wilson instead preferred James Duncan of the A. F. of L., who had been a member of the Root Mission (Daniels Diary).
[94] Spargo to John A. Gade, Chief of the Division of Russian Affairs, with a notation by Gade, August 3, 1920, Colby Papers. See Radosh, "Spargo and Wilson's Russian Policy." The Russian Embassy, on March 22, 1920, had advised Polk that a general statement of policy would be timely (*For. Rel., 1920* **3**: pp. 451-453).
[95] Memorandum by Davis, Colby Papers.

British authorities declared that they could not furnish troops, but many volunteers apparently were available if Poland could pay them, the Polish Legation inquired whether the United States could make funds available in a complicated scheme whereby Poland would compensate Great Britain for the volunteers by assuming part of the English war debt to America on liberal terms. Neither Davis nor Colby viewed that as feasible since Congress probably would not grant the necessary authorization.[96]

It was decided to make a full statement of American policy in the form of a reply to the Italian inquiry. Undersecretary Davis advised Colby that it should advocate the preservation of both Polish and Russian territorial integrity, and thereby indirectly to criticize Polish aggression in seeking control of areas east of the ethnic or Curzon Line. The reasons for non-recognition of the Soviet regime should be strongly stated, and it should be suggested tactfully to the Allies that attempts to dismember Russia would serve merely to crystallize support around the Bolsheviks. The Bolsheviks should not be recognized because they did not express the popular will and represented rule only by a self-constituted "murderous minority"; it "is utterly impossible for two systems based on such diametrically opposed principles [Bolshevism versus democracy] to work in peace and harmony." [97]

Colby wrote the first two introductory paragraphs of the resulting note, followed by the insertion with a few changes of the long main section drawn from Spargo's memorandum of July 31; the concluding two paragraphs were also Colby's work. He forwarded the finished note to the President with the remark that it was long and had one major weakness: "It is impossible to say what we will *do*, if anything," about the Polish crisis. Wilson approved it with the notation,

[96] Davis-Colby exchange, August 6, 1920, *For. Rel., 1920* **3:** pp. 386, 387.
[97] Davis to Colby, August 7, 1920, Davis Papers. Also see memorandum by John A. Gade to Davis, August 9, 1920, Colby Papers.

"This seems to me excellent and sufficient."[98] As noted before, Wilson subsequently praised the note to a reporter as entirely Colby's phraseology, though he stated that he and the Secretary had discussed its contents on several occasions and the ideas were his own.[99]

The note to the Italian Ambassador, Baron Camillo Avezzano, was cast in the form of a response to Italy's intimation that it would welcome an expression of American views on the Polish crisis. Colby affirmed the interest of the United States in the preservation of Poland's integrity, and that it did not object to efforts to arrange a Polish-Soviet armistice. However, the American government was opposed to any attempt to broaden armistice negotiations into a general conference that would recognize the Bolshevik regime and settle the Russian problem on the basis of dismemberment. America had great faith in the Russian people and their future, and was confident that they would surmount the present crisis: "Until that time shall arrive the United States feels that friendship and honor require that Russia's interests must be generously protected, and that, as far as possible, all decisions of vital importance to it . . . be held in abeyance." For those reasons, American recognition had been withheld from the Baltic states and the republics proclaimed in South Russia. Colby averred American sympathy with Allied desires to solve European problems peacefully, but he declared an inability to perceive how recognition of the Soviet regime would contribute to that goal. Relations with the Bolshevik authorities should be confined within the narrow limits of armistice arrangements:

> It is not possible for the Government of the United States to recognize the present rulers of Russia as a government with which the relations common to friendly governments can be maintained.

[98] Colby to Wilson, August 9, 1920, Colby Papers.
[99] Confidential interview with William W. Hawkins of Scripps-Howard, September 27, 1920, in the Colby Papers.

This conviction has nothing to do with any particular political or social structure which the Russian people themselves may see fit to embrace. It rests upon a wholly different set of facts. These facts . . . have convinced the Government of the United States . . . that the existing regime in Russia is based upon the negation of every principle of honor and good faith, and every usage and convention, underlying the whole structure of international law; the negation, in short, of every principle upon which it is possible to base harmonious and trustful relations, whether of nations or of individuals.[100]

Communist ideology and practice meant that "no compact or agreement made with a non-Bolshevist government can have any moral force for them." The Bolshevik regime sought to instigate and encourage revolutionary movements in other countries, working through the Third International or Comintern which was directed by the small group controlling the Soviet government. Therefore assurances that diplomatic privileges would not be abused were worthless. Soviet leaders had boasted that their promises of non-interference in the affairs of other nations would not restrain the activities of Comintern agents who in fact would be aided by Soviet diplomats. "Inevitably, therefore, the diplomatic service of the Bolshevist Government would become a channel for intrigues and the propaganda of revolt. . . ." There could be no common ground of confidence, respect or trust: "We cannot recognize . . . a government which is determined and bound to conspire against our institutions; whose diplomats will be the agitators of dangerous revolt; whose spokesmen say that they sign agreements with no intention of keeping them." Colby concluded the note with the comment that the United States would regard with satisfaction a declaration by the Allied and Associated Powers that the territorial integrity and the true boundaries of Russia would be respected, to include the whole of the former Russian empire except for Finland, ethnic Poland, and such territory as by agreement

[100] Colby to Avezzano, August 10, 1920, *For. Rel., 1920* **3**: pp. 463-468.

might become part of an Armenian state. The aspirations of the Finns, Poles, and Armenians were viewed as legitimate, having been forcibly annexed to Russia in the past, and their independence would not constitute an act of aggression against Russian territorial rights. With these exceptions, the Allies should declare that all foreign troops presently on Russian territory should be withdrawn, and no transgressions by Poland, Finland, or others would be permitted. Only in that way could Bolshevism be deprived of its false appeal to Russian nationalism.

As one student of this period has commented, the Colby note was based firmly on principle in regard to non-recognition and was "a harsh position, and a negative one" that ignored questions of debts and claims for the larger issues as the American government viewed them. It thereby commanded a measure of understanding and even respect from Soviet authorities that was not accorded to the non-recognition statements by the other powers.[101] Yet as Colby had admitted to Wilson, the American note failed to state any positive action to resolve the Polish-Soviet conflict or, he could have added, the larger Russian problem. While Great Britain and France were actively involved, the United States was not; it could only offer the general advice of a hands-off policy until the Russian people themselves should solve their internal problems. Although Colby and Wilson were confident that the Bolshevik regime could not long survive —a view encouraged by Spargo—the August 10 note formalized a policy of non-recognition that was to become increasingly unrealistic as the Soviet government solidified its authority. Time also revealed that non-recognition did not prevent Communist propaganda and activities in the United States; an open society could not easily protect its institutions against subversive endeavors. All non-recognition actually achieved, it would seem, was to make American

---

[101] Kennan, *Russia and the West under Lenin and Stalin*, pp. 206-207.

policy toward Soviet Russia more rigid and unresponsive when it was continued during the 1920's, thereby depriving the United States of an opportunity to gather direct information about Russian internal developments and to influence the international behavior of the Soviets. As for Colby's declaration against dismemberment, the United States under the Harding administration adjusted to reality and recognized the independence of Lithuania, Latvia, and Estonia in 1922.

The Colby note was favorably received by the American press. Wilson was generally credited as the real author of what was described as a note "admirable in contents and admirable in form." [102] Some commentators praised the statement as moral support of Poland and an indication to the Russian people that it was time to throw off the Bolshevik yoke. A few journals, however, viewed the declaration as negative and meaningless in terms of the actual Soviet menace to Poland and American non-involvement, in contrast to the more positive efforts of the Allies to cope with the crisis. Historian Robert J. Kerner, a Russian specialist who had been a member of the peace delegation and was teaching at the University of Missouri, described the note as a significant support for Russian territorial integrity within its proper ethnic boundaries. Kerner wrote that Wilson had raised the problem to the high moral level of justice and the happiness of the Russian people.[103] The prevailing opinion was summed up a few months later in an editorial in the New York *Times:* "The true policy toward the Soviet Government, the wise and sound policy, was laid down by the firm hand of Secretary Colby. . . ."[104]

The reactions of foreign governments were mixed. France declared its complete concurrence, while Czechoslovakia agreed but expressed opposition to any military intervention

[102] *Literary Digest* **66** (August 21, 1920): pp. 13-14.
[103] Robert J. Kerner, "Colby's Challenge," New York *Times,* August 15, 1920.
[104] November 18, 1920, *ibid.*

in Russia and emphasized the importance to all Europe of resuming economic relations with Russia as soon as possible.[105] Great Britain and Italy evidenced little enthusiasm for a common policy toward the Soviets. Lord Curzon complained to his ambassador in Paris that France seemed to have spurned its British ally for the undependable Americans.[106] Geddes later reported that French Ambassador Jusserand had frightened Colby about Red activities and was trying to persuade the State Department formally to protest against any Anglo-Soviet trade agreement.[107] The British Ambassador informed Colby and Undersecretary Davis, on February 21, 1921, that although he personally concurred in the wisdom of the American policy, his government could not follow the same course because of the critical attitude of organized labor in England and on the continent.[108]

When George Chicherin, the Soviet Foreign Minister, denied that his government had ever stated that it would not observe its pledges, Colby answered via the press by citing contrary statements by Lenin and other Bolsheviks.[109] Chicherin publicly protested against Colby's note to Italy and, after declaring that Soviet Russia deemed friendly relations with all other existing governments to be necessary, he urged the American people to reject the Secretary's

[105] *For. Rel., 1920* **3**: 469-470, 472-473. The State Department urged France to take a more liberal stand on reparations and enforcement of the Versailles Treaty, in order to preclude possible German cooperation with the Bolsheviks. Doubt was expressed about French recognition of General Peter N. Wrangel in south Russia, but the department admitted it lacked sufficient information to pass judgment (*ibid.* **3**: p. 471). Colby publicly praised the French government for supporting the American position on Russia (August 19, 1920, New York *Times*).
[106] Curzon to the Earl of Derby, August 15, 1920, *Documents on British Foreign Policy* **11**: p. 489.
[107] Geddes to Curzon, November 25, 1920, F.O.115/2628/Russia 12 (13).
[108] S.D.File 462.00R29/3511, Archives.
[109] August 18, 1920, Colby Papers. See Louis Fischer, *The Soviets in World Affairs* (2 v., London & New York, 1930) **1**: pp. 306-312. For a general survey of this period in Soviet-American relations, consult Frederick Lewis Schuman, *American Policy toward Russia since 1917* (New York, 1928), pp. 175-183.

"short-sighted policy." [110] A copy of Chicherin's note to Italy was delivered to the State Department on October 4 by Ludwig Martens, the unrecognized Soviet representative. A mixture of revolutionary jargon and appeals to American businessmen assumed to be interested in Russian trade, Chicherin's rejoinder spurned Colby's defense of the integrity of the old empire as based on misinformation, asserted that if Russia presently were not a workers' state it would be under a bourgeois government identified with the world's dominant financial interests including its most powerful element, American capitalists, and accused Colby of trying to establish control by these capitalistic groups in Russia. The United States was against the independence of certain former Russian territories, Chicherin sneered, only because British rather than American capital was entrenched in those areas. Charges of bad faith were denied and the desire for normal relations reasserted, because the Soviet government recognized that in America and other countries the workers were not yet convinced of the need to conquer their governments.[111]

Within the limits of non-involvement dictated by the political situation in the United States, the State Department encouraged the end of warfare between Poland and the Soviets. When a group of Polish-Americans appealed to Colby for aid to save Poland from the Bolsheviks, he replied that nothing could be done by the executive and they should appeal to public opinion and the Congress.[112] Ambassador Wallace was instructed by Colby, on August

[110] September 17, 1920, New York *Times*.
[111] *For. Rel., 1920* **3**: pp. 474-478. The State Department urged the Chinese government not to abolish Russia's extraterritoriality and other rights in China, as the Bolsheviks had suggested. China agreed to respect other rights, while extraterritoriality temporarily lapsed. A joint effort by the interested powers failed to alter China's position (*ibid.* **1**: pp. 763-783). Martens was ordered deported on December 16, 1920 (*ibid.* **3**: pp. 478-480). See Thomas A. Bailey, *America Faces Russia* (Ithaca, 1950), pp. 247-250; and Robert Paul Browder, *The Origins of Soviet-American Diplomacy* (Princeton, New Jersey, 1953), pp. 13-18.
[112] August 19, 1920, New York *Times*.

21, to express to the Council of Ambassadors at Paris the hope that the transportation of supplies to Poland would be facilitated, as long as such aid was "used only in defending Polish territory and not to make it possible for Poland again to ... invade Russia." [113] The American Chargé in Warsaw also was instructed to make clear American friendship and admiration for Polish gallantry in defending their capital, but to express the desire for a termination of the conflict and disapproval of any offensive war program against Russia.[114] In Washington's opinion, the recent Polish invasion had rallied Russian nationalist support behind the Bolshevik regime; a show of moderation on Poland's part, such as a declaration of intent to remain within the Curzon Line, would be the best way of coping with the Bolsheviks.

When Danzig workers refused to transport vital aid to Poland through that port, Great Britain and France decided to dispatch warships there. It was suggested that the United States might cooperate in a similar manner to fulfill the purposes of the Versailles Treaty. Colby declined because the Treaty had not been approved by the Senate, but he stated that a warship would be sent to aid the Americans resident in Danzig, a type of parallel action acceptable to the British.[115] The President was very annoyed at this decision by the State and Navy Departments, which had been made without consulting him. When Daniels explained that it had been requested by Colby to protect American citizens, Wilson exclaimed, "Rats," and that such an excuse was always used to send ships that should not be sent.[116] Wilson wrote Colby of his surprise at the action. The Secretary managed to mollify his anger by apologizing for non-consultation: "Let me repeat, my dear Mr.

---

[113] *For. Rel., 1920* **3**: p. 391.
[114] *Ibid.* **3**: pp. 391-392.
[115] Wallace to Colby, August 24, and Colby to Wallace, August 24, 1920, *ibid.* **3**: pp. 393-394, 394-395, 395-396.
[116] August 31, and September 1, 1920, Daniels Diary.

President, my sincere regret that I did not give the matter sufficient reflection to perceive the propriety and importance of submitting this matter for your approval." [117] Wilson replied, on the same day, that he would accept their judgment but he wanted to be kept informed of all problems relating to the unratified Treaty. The vessel was not sent after all, as later information indicated that its arrival would be misunderstood as a sign of American support of Polish expansionism.

The Polish government defended its expansionist course to the State Department as necessary resistance to Bolshevik aggression. Warsaw declared that an artificially drawn boundary—the Curzon Line—which the Soviets allegedly did not respect in their military activities should not be permitted to interfere with Polish operations.[118] Undersecretary Davis, acting for Colby, instructed Ambassador Wallace that it should be understood that Polish claims to territory east of the ethnic boundary set by the Supreme Council would not be prejudiced at a time when a unified Russia could be consulted, but the Department was of the opinion that strategic excuses should not be used to justify further Polish advances. As the Treaty had not been approved by the Senate, the American government was unable to participate in negotiations over Danzig; for that same reason no aid could be supplied and it was believed that Poland should adopt reasonable measures to terminate the war with the Soviets.[119] Reports from the American Minister in Warsaw that France was encouraging advances beyond the Curzon Line caused Colby to direct that, if asked, the American views opposing such action should be conveyed informally to the Polish government.[120] A successful Polish counter-offensive led to an armistice in October,

[117] Colby to Wilson, September 1, 1920, Colby Papers.
[118] *For. Rel., 1920* **3**: pp. 397-398.
[119] Davis to Wallace, August 31, 1920, *ibid.* **3**: pp. 399-400.
[120] *Ibid.* **3**: pp. 401-405.

1920. The conflict was finally settled by the 1921 Treaty of Riga, when the Soviet government accepted Polish boundaries drawn 150 to 200 miles east of the Curzon Line. In accordance with its previous policy, the State Department did not recognize the validity of the boundary agreement.

On Spargo's advice, Colby did attempt to develop a more positive American policy toward Russia. The Secretary was persuaded that the Bolshevik regime was on the verge of a collapse, having lost the support of the Russian peasantry, and he predicted an early demise that would open the way to some form of genuinely representative self-government. His remarks aroused great interest in diplomatic and political circles in Washington.[121] Spargo suggested a plan for the Social Democratic Prime Minister of Sweden, Hjalmar Branting, to propose a solution based on a relinquishment of the Bolshevik dictatorship, the formation and diplomatic recognition of a new Russian government, and western promises of non-interference and economic aid for Russia. According to Spargo's account, Wilson approved and Branting was enthusiastic, but objections within his Cabinet and its collapse in October, 1920, doomed the project, and with it Colby's effort to formulate a more constructive Russian policy.[122]

[121] October 22 and 24, 1920, New York *Times*.

[122] Spargo to Colby, August 25, 1920, Colby Papers; and Spargo, "Colby," pp. 206-208. See Radosh, "Spargo and Wilson's Russian Policy." President Wilson on November 3, 1920, wrote Prime Minister Lloyd George a private letter in reply to his personal letter of August 5, 1920. Wilson reiterated his view that "Bolshevism would have burned out long ago if left alone. . . ." He was opposed to any trade discussions with the Soviets or to consideration of diplomatic recognition as serving no useful purpose and merely tending to prolong them in power. As for Poland, he feared that "their enthusiasm following temporary military successes may lead to insistence upon territorial arrangements which will be a source of future trouble." Wilson also discussed the British war debts to America, that he insisted must be repaid, and expressed confidence that regardless of the outcome of the November elections, he had faith that the American people after the confusions of the immediate present had passed would "cooperate unselfishly for the betterment of the world. . . ." S.D.File 72.72119/12200, Archives, and the Wilson Papers.

III. East Asia: Anglo-American Cooperation

COLBY FELL HEIR to three major and interrelated Far Eastern problems: the consortium, Japanese expansionism on the mainland of Asia, and the immigration question. All of these were issues of long standing, and it was not surprising that during his brief secretaryship Colby was to solve only one, the consortium, and that merely in a formal sense. Yet he was able to further Anglo-American cooperation in the Far East and to make some progress toward moderating the Japanese thrust in Manchuria and Siberia. He thereby contributed to the Pacific treaty system that was to emerge from the 1921-1922 Washington conference.

1.

The torturous negotiations for the consortium began in July, 1918, when Lansing had proposed to the principal Allied powers the formation of a new international bankers' group, composed of British, French, Japanese, and American bankers, to advance needed funds to the Chinese republic. Current financial loan options were to be turned over to the proposed four-power consortium. The American plan also included all industrial loans within its scope.[1] Lansing's unannounced purpose was to aid China in the

[1] *Papers Relating to the Foreign Relations of the United States, 1918* (Washington, 1930), pp. 176-177, 180-181. For a detailed account, see Frederick V. Field, *American Participation in the China Consortium* (Chicago, 1931), pp. 142-165.

defense of its integrity, prevent its reliance upon Japanese sources alone for financial loans, and in effect to break down all existing spheres of influence.[2] The Japanese government particularly was reluctant to bring industrial activity under the proposed consortium, but the State Department insisted. A new Japanese ministry seemed to be more cooperative, however, and in February and March, 1919, tentative agreement was reached to include both financial and industrial loans.[3] A meeting of the banking representatives of the powers involved was held in Paris in May, and it was agreed in principle that all future business should be handled by the consortium and all existing activities and options brought under its jurisdiction. A place was to be reserved for Russian participation, and Belgium was to be given favorable consideration for membership after the plan was in operation. Wilson approved the proposal with its safeguards designed to protect China from violation of its sovereignty.[4]

Subsequent negotiations revealed that Japan was still reluctant to include all activities in China within the consortium. It sought to exclude Japanese rights and options in Manchuria and Mongolia, on the grounds of Japan's special interests in those areas, recognized by the Allied Powers and referred to in the 1917 Lansing-Ishii Agreement.[5] T. W. Lamont of J. P. Morgan and Company conferred with Lansing in Paris on the problem; the Secretary of State was inclined to inform Japan that the United States

---

[2] Polk to the Chargé in Peking, August 10, 1918, *For. Rel., 1918*, p. 188.

[3] *Ibid.*, pp. 191-192, 193-196; and *For. Rel., 1919* 1: pp. 423-433.

[4] *For. Rel., 1919* 1: pp. 435-436; and Lansing to Wilson, May 26, and Wilson to Lansing, May 27, 1919, Wilson Papers. A Japanese effort to have one of its nationals appointed financial adviser to China was opposed by the State Department in view of the negotiations on the consortium. Ambassador Kikujiro Ishii averred that Lansing had agreed to that step in May, 1918, and, when Lansing failed to remember giving his approval, professed such great embarrassment that he announced he would not return to America after his forthcoming leave of absence in Japan. *Ibid.* 1: pp. 556-566.

[5] *Ibid.* 1: pp. 451-453.

would try to organize the consortium without Japan's participation if it insisted on excluding those areas.[6] Although the American bankers were willing to participate in only a three-power group, their French and British counterparts were reluctant to exclude Japan except as a last resort. The French government agreed that the Japanese position in regard to Manchuria and Mongolia was wholly inadmissible, but expressed fear that exclusion of Japan from the consortium would isolate that power and perhaps force it to seek a rapprochement with Germany on Chinese affairs.[7] Lansing informed the Japanese government of the impossibility of exempting any area from the consortium, but he pointed out that there was no intention of interfering with purely private industrial enterprises but only of reserving all loans made to China for any purpose to the international group.[8]

Lansing persisted in his determination to organize the group without Japanese participation if necessary, and President Wilson concurred.[9] The Chinese government, however, expressed fear of probable Japanese hostility and urged that negotiations be transferred to Washington; Britain and France also took the position that exclusion was inadvisable.[10] A British proposed compromise to accept the Japanese reservation in regard to Manchuria but not Inner Mongolia was rejected by Lansing. The Secretary denied that the Lansing-Ishii Agreement had implied a Japanese monopoly or priority of industrial and economic opportunities in those areas and declared that if the consortium were to recognize spheres of influence it would be a calamity for China and for the other interested powers.

[6] June 20, 1919, Lansing Desk Diary; and *For. Rel., 1919* 1: pp. 453-455.
[7] S.D.File 893.41/4900, Archives; and *For. Rel., 1919* 1: pp. 459-461, 470.
[8] Lansing Memorandum to the Japanese Embassy, July 30, 1919, S.D.File 893.41/2383, Archives.
[9] August 27, 1919, Lansing Desk Diary; and *For. Rel., 1919* 1: pp. 480-482.
[10] *For. Rel., 1919* 1: pp. 484-492.

Moreover, there was no intention of interference with existing Japanese enterprises in Manchuria and Mongolia but only of pooling projects not yet actually underway. The United States would accept a Japanese reservation of existing activities but would not recognize a geographical reservation. Lansing hoped that Britain and France would cooperate with the State Department but he warned that, if not, the Department was prepared to proceed unilaterally.[11] It seems clear that Lansing still believed that only a firm stand would strengthen the forces for moderation in Japan and lay the basis for genuine cooperation in a stabilized Far East.

The impasse had not been wholly resolved when Colby took charge of the State Department, but the firm American position was beginning to modify Japan's attitude. A Japanese compromise formula to exempt specific enterprises contained a larger number than expected but nevertheless was acceptable to the American government; however, the formula seemed to the State Department to be superfluous and to imply a special status for Manchuria and Mongolia.[12] Although the United States had received with "hearty gratification" Japan's denial of any claim to exclusive economic or political rights in those areas, the American reply expressed great disappointment at the ambiguous phraseology of the Japanese formula. Japan's proposal seemed to indicate a desire to exclude the Anglo-American-French banking groups from economic developments in South Manchuria and Inner Mongolia. Japan should be able to rely upon the good faith of the other members of the consortium not to interfere with legitimate

[11] Lansing to Ambassador Davis, October 11, and Memorandum to the Japanese Embassy, October 28, 1919, *ibid.* 1: pp. 493-496, 497-499. Lansing told Ambassador-designate Viscount Grey that Britain and the United States should cooperate to restrain an aggressive Japan, and that an open door in Manchuria and Inner Mongolia would be enough of a benefit for Japan.—Grey to Curzon, October 10 and 22, 1919, *Documents on British Foreign Policy* 6: pp. 766, 794.

[12] Polk to Davis, March 6, 1920, *For. Rel., 1920* 1: pp. 503-505.

enterprises and the State Department hoped that the formula would be abandoned.[13] Accepting a proposal by Roland S. Morris, the Ambassador to Japan, and Lamont for an exchange of statements between the bankers excluding certain projects of special interest to Japan, the Japanese government withdrew its formula and expressed satisfaction with the American reassurances about the operations of the consortium.[14]

After a further delay, Japan in early May, 1920, approved the consortium essentially as it had been proposed nearly two years earlier by the United States. Great Britain and France had cooperated closely with the United States in persuading the Japanese authorities to abandon their demands for special treatment.[15] Although Wilson pronounced himself as "sincerely glad," [16] the consortium in action was to achieve nothing of importance. The Chinese government revealed little eagerness to borrow through the consortium, apparently preferring to arrange loans independently with private financiers.[17] The chief significance of the protracted negotiations was their implication of vigorous American support of the Open Door and as a factor in encouraging a more cautious, moderate policy on the part of Japan.

2.

The State Department obtained a large measure of British support in its determined effort to prevent the Russian-owned Chinese Eastern Railway in Manchuria from coming

[13] *Ibid.* **1**: pp. 512-513. The State Department also expressed its inability to perceive why certain railroad projects in the area should be constructed exclusively by Japanese firms.
[14] *Ibid.* **1**: pp. 519-526.
[15] *Ibid.* **1**: pp. 536-538.
[16] Colby to Wilson, May 8, and Wilson to Colby, May 9, 1920, Wilson and Colby Papers; and *For. Rel., 1920* **1**: pp. 539-541. The agreement was signed on October 15, 1920.
[17] *For. Rel., 1920* **1**: pp. 671-672.

under exclusive Japanese control. At Wilson's instruction, Davis had a frank talk with Ambassador Geddes on April 20. After relating information that officials in the British Embassy in Tokyo were undercutting Anglo-American cooperation by expressing sympathy with Japanese expansionism, Davis warned that England should not try to play America off against Japan. Geddes expressed amazement at Davis' information and reassured him of complete British cooperation.[18] The British Foreign Office concurred with the view of the department that firm pressure would bring Japanese agreement on the consortium and related questions, but it was convinced that in regard to all these problems, including renewal of the Anglo-Japanese Alliance (due to expire in 1921), "it is better to cooperate with the Japanese as allies than to take the contrary course." [19] Colby expressed gratitude at the Anglo-American "complete accord." [20] Both governments were concerned about the status of the Chinese Eastern Railway, where clashes were reported along its tracks between Japanese and Chinese soldiers. In response to a suggestion from the British Embassy, Colby tentatively proposed that after the Technical Board established by the 1919 agreement had expired, the railway should be turned over to China as trustee for the Russian owners.[21]

In view of these disturbing clashes of interest and principle in the Far East, the American government preferred that the Anglo-Japanese Alliance not be renewed. Secretary Colby informed the London Embassy on March 26 that he hoped the alliance would not be extended, as it would have an unfortunate effect.[22] Yet an analysis by the Division of Far Eastern Affairs concluded that although

[18] S.D.File 711.41/128, Archives.
[19] Davis to Colby, April 21, 1920, *For. Rel., 1920* 1: pp. 531-532.
[20] Colby to Davis, April 23, 1920, *ibid.* 1: p. 534.
[21] Colby to Davis, April 26, 1920, *ibid.* 1: pp. 685-686.
[22] S.D.File 744.9411/24, Archives.

the alliance had benefited Japan more than Great Britain, the British government could hardly terminate it without antagonizing Japan. Therefore, despite an awareness in Great Britain of the fact that the alliance tended to deflect its policy away from that pursued by the United States in the Far East, the British government probably would not take the initiative in proposing revisions. The division recommended that the department informally suggest changes in the treaty designed to reduce British support of Japanese spheres of influence and to remove the United States as a potential target of the alliance.[23] With the approval of Colby and Wilson, Ambassador Davis in London was asked whether it would be advisable to suggest that any renewal of the alliance should include clauses incorporating the provision relating to the Open Door from the Lansing-Ishii Agreement, and the exclusion of the United States from the application of the alliance on the grounds that it had signed a Bryan "cooling-off" pact with Great Britain in 1914. The latter contention was designed to comply with the terms of the 1911 renewal exempting application of the alliance to countries which had signed arbitration treaties with one of the signatories (unfortunately the Senate had wrecked the Anglo-American Arbitration Treaty signed in 1911). The consortium negotiations had revealed an Anglo-American community of interest, the Department's inquiry noted, and it was hoped that it would be reflected in the new version of the Anglo-Japanese Alliance. Because Japanese foreign policy appeared to be unstable, the Department also thought it wise to renew the alliance only for a term of five instead of ten years.[24] Ambassador Davis subsequently reported that he had informally conveyed these views to the British Foreign Office and had received assurances that they would be considered—

[23] Memorandum of April 28, 1920, S.D.File 741.9411/26, *ibid*.
[24] Polk to Davis, May 10, 1920, *For. Rel., 1920* **2**: pp. 680-681.

especially to make clear that the United States was not the target—when the alliance was redrafted.[25]

In fact, there was wide agreement within the British Foreign Office and diplomatic service that the Anglo-Japanese Alliance had outlived most of its usefulness. Victor Wellesley, the Foreign Office's Assistant Secretary for Far Eastern Affairs, in a memorandum on June 1, apropos of soundings from the American Embassy, analyzed the alliance as having "notoriously failed" to restrain Japan. Gradually, he wrote, the alliance has "come to be almost diametrically opposed to the best interests of not only Great Britain and the United States but of China herself. . . ."[26] To perpetuate it would only be a marriage of convenience. Preferable, in his view, would be a "tripartite agreement" among Britain, America, and Japan that would avoid affronting Japan or isolating her and yet would be capable of restraining her expansionist tendencies: "The closer our cooperation with America, the wider the open door [in China]." The key question, of course, was if the American government, facing popular anti-British and anti-Japanese currents, would "dare to face the music" involved in a tripartite understanding.

The issue of renewal was a delicate one for Britain, caught between American wishes that it lapse and Japan's reliance upon it for prestige and security.[27] Britain's new Minister to China, Sir Beilby F. Alston, was sent to Washington in late July by the Foreign Office to confer with Geddes and the State Department. At a dinner where Colby was present, Alston discovered that the Secretary agreed with his remarks that the only satisfactory solution in the Far East would have to be built upon "a clear understand-

---

[25] Davis to Colby, June 7, 1920, *ibid.* **2**: p. 682.
[26] *Documents on British Foreign Policy* **14**: pp. 32-36.
[27] As a dispatch from Geddes to Curzon, June 5, 1920, and attached minutes made clear (F.O.371/5359/F1043/199/23).

ing and intimate cooperation" between England and America, perhaps taking the form of an agreement to maintain adequate naval power in the Pacific to restrain Japan.[28] Subsequently, Alston advised his superiors that he was not suggesting an aggressive anti-Japanese policy but an Anglo-American understanding—a treaty would be unnecessary. He reported that Colby had assured him that any administration in Washington would favor such cooperation, which caused Sir Eyre Crowe of the Foreign Office to comment on the report: "I wish I could share Sir B. Alston's robust faith in America's 'co-operation' in China or elsewhere. But I see no objection to making further efforts to gain it."[29]

Colby was an enthusiastic convert to Anglo-American collaboration, to the agreeable surprise of British officials who had initially viewed him as a pro-Irish cipher. When Colby's appointment as Secretary of State had been announced, in late February of 1920, the British Chargé in Washington had reported the general appraisal that the new Secretary was unqualified for his post and that he was inclined to be anti-British in sentiment.[30] A few months in office persuaded British observers that they had been wrong. As one minute by a Foreign Office official on a dispatch from Ambassador Geddes expressed it, Colby was "now well disposed" toward Britain.[31] Geddes relayed, on May 28, a recent conversation he had had with Colby:

> He told me that he would regard it as the greatest possible achievement of his period of tenure of the office of Secretary of State if, during it, an agreement should be arrived at which would dispel

---

[28] Memorandum by Sir B. F. Alston, August 1, 1920, *Documents on British Foreign Policy* **14**: pp. 77-80.
[29] *Ibid.* **14**: pp. 81-86.
[30] F.O.371/4576/A932,A1342/712/45.
[31] Geddes to Curzon, May 21, 1920, and minute, F.O.371/4601/A3493/3493/45. Irish-American spokesmen expressed great disappointment when Colby as Secretary of State failed to support their cause.

forever the idea or possibility of naval or commercial rivalry . . . between the English-speaking peoples.[32]

Geddes was briefly swept up in the optimism about an Anglo-American *entente*. As he reported, on October 18, "there is now for the first time since 1776 some chance of arriving at a working agreement with this country which it will observe and honour." [33] After the elections, however, the apparently greatly discouraged Ambassador informed the Foreign Office that while most thoughtful Americans would welcome an exchange of identic notes between Britain, the United States, and Japan affirming the Open Door in China, and the conclusion of an Anglo-American naval understanding to curb Japan in the Pacific, the Senate was not likely to approve anything resembling an Anglo-American alliance, and an informal agreement could not be relied upon to last indefinitely. About the best that could be hoped for, in view of the American electoral system, was a four-year agreement. Therefore he recommended renewal of the Anglo-Japanese Alliance, but without its objectionable features, and the seeking of an executive agreement with the incoming Harding administration.[34] "Japan," he wrote, "may not have proved to be an ideal Ally, but it is doubtful if America would be more easy to work with in double harness, at least in her present frame of mind." [35]

Curzon was fully aware of the difficulty of obtaining a practical agreement with America and apprehensive of offending Japan while Britain was weak navally in the Pacific.[36] Yet the Foreign Office's Anglo-Japanese Alliance Committee unanimously recommended non-renewal of the

---

[32] F.O.371/4601/A3755/3493/45.
[33] F.O.371/4612/A7615/7615/45.
[34] Geddes to Curzon, November 15, 1920, *Documents on British Foreign Policy* **14**: pp. 177-178.
[35] Geddes to Curzon, December 3, 1920, *ibid.* **14**: pp. 187-189.
[36] *Ibid.* **6**: p. 880.

alliance.[37] As the Wilson administration left office, British official thought ran along the lines of either replacing the alliance with a tripartite settlement in the Pacific and an Anglo-American naval agreement, or if that failed revision of the alliance to comply with the League Covenant and American desires.

While the subject of the Anglo-Japanese Alliance was just beginning to be discussed, the State Department reacted favorably to a proposal from the Russian Embassy in Washington that a special international trusteeship committee for the Chinese Eastern Railway be established, to be financed by loans from the consortium or from other sources.[38] Informal discussions between Ambassador Davis and the Foreign Office revealed that the British would prefer a continuation of the 1919 Inter-Allied Agreement on the railways, joint Sino-Japanese protection of the Chinese Eastern, and financing by the consortium (perhaps only by the American and Japanese bankers as the English group had been delayed in organizing). The State Department was pleased at the degree of Anglo-American agreement, though in the light of past difficulties it wanted the operations of Japanese troops along the railway restricted to emergencies.[39]

Further exchanges brought the two governments closer to an agreed policy. The proposed "international bankruptcy commission" for the Chinese Eastern Railway (hereafter referred to as the C.E.R.) was also discussed with France. Colby instructed the American Chargé in Tokyo to treat confidentially information about the proposal, only to discover that the British Foreign Office was keeping Japan fully informed even at the exploratory stage, in the belief that it was wise to avoid possible Japanese irritation

[37] F.O.371/6671/F91/63/23; and *Documents on British Foreign Policy* 14: pp. 221-227.
[38] Colby to the Chargé in Tokyo, May 17, 1920, *For. Rel., 1920* 1: pp. 690-691.
[39] *Ibid.* 1: pp. 691-694.

at later being confronted with an accomplished scheme.[40] Discussions between the British Ambassador in Tokyo and the Japanese Foreign Minister revealed that Japan viewed an immediate consortium loan to the C.E.R. as inexpedient because of Japanese internal political developments. Moreover, the French government was not eager to finance the railway by paying its share for past military use of the system, and French interests in the Russo-Asiatic Bank raised objections to the proposal of an international bankruptcy commission.[41]

While discussions continued pending Ambassador Morris' return to Washington from Tokyo to participate in the conversations, Colby had a sharp protest lodged against Japanese occupation of the northern or Russian half of the island of Sakhalin. Drafted by Norman Davis pursuant to Wilson's direction, the note found unconvincing the Japanese defense of the occupation as retaliation to attacks on Japanese civilians and troops by roving Bolshevik bands on the mainland of Siberia. The occupation was declared to be at variance with the previous Japanese-American agreement on the purpose of military efforts in Siberia, and concern was expressed at such "encroachments upon Russian territory." The United States "cannot participate in the announced decision of your Government with regard to Sakhalien, nor can it recognize the occupation of said territory by any non-Russian authority." [42] Colby earlier had told Ambassador Geddes that personally he viewed the incidents cited by Japan as "fake massacres" or at least as instigated by Japan.[43] The Secretary described President

[40] *Ibid.* **1**: pp. 695, 696.
[41] *Ibid.* **1**: pp. 697-698, 700, 704.
[42] Colby to Wilson, July 16, 1918, Colby Papers; and Colby to the Japanese Ambassador, July 16, 1920, *For. Rel., 1920* **3**: pp. 517-519.
[43] Geddes to Curzon, July 11, 1920, *Documents on British Foreign Policy* **14**: pp. 70-71; and Geddes to Curzon, July 12, 1920, F.O.115/2628/Russia 20 (8).

Wilson as convinced that the United States must serve as trustee for a disunited Russia and determined to compel Japan to evacuate the occupied areas. Japan would not "show fight," but British cooperation was requested in halting her expansion.

Japan did not retreat, contrary to the expectations of Wilson and Colby. In its defense of the Sakhalin occupation, the Tokyo government again invoked the right of retaliation under international law and practice, and explained that Japanese public opinion was outraged at recent incidents in Siberia.[44] Because of the delicacy of its relations with Japan, the British government did not join the United States in protesting the occupation, contenting itself merely with an inquiry.[45] Not until 1925 was Japan to conclude a treaty with Soviet Russia for the evacuation of its troops.

Early in August conversations in Washington between British Ambassador Geddes, Morris, Norman Davis, and Colby, saw the emergence of a plan to continue international control of the C.E.R. until it could revert to its original owners under Russian control. The railway would be supervised by China, Japan, Great Britain, France, and the United States, and policed by Chinese forces; financing of the C.E.R. possibly could be arranged by using Russian gold paid as war indemnities to Germany at Brest-Litovsk and since recovered by the Allies. The British Foreign Office agreed to the first point and tentatively to the second, although it noted the danger that Russian Bolshevism posed in the area and thought Japan might accept the scheme more readily if its troops were permitted to participate in guarding the C.E.R. It remained for the British, however, to remind the State Department that legally the recovered

[44] *For. Rel. 1920* **3**: pp. 522-524.
[45] *Documents on British Foreign Policy* **14**: pp. 77, 95.

gold still belonged to Russia. It was thought advisable, therefore, to arrange financing of the C.E.R. through the consortium.[46]

Information from an intercepted British telegram indicated that while the British government spoke of cooperation with the United States, at the same time it was expressing sympathy with Japan's position in the Far East—apparently this referred to the occupation of northern Sakhalin. During a Cabinet discussion of this intelligence, President Wilson commented that it was a typically English reaction of sympathy for anyone following its own example of "grab everything it can."[47] The evidence indicates that the British government in fact did agree with the American position that Japan should not be allowed to dominate the C.E.R. or to impair further the Open Door in China. Britain, however, appreciated Japanese concern with the menace of Bolshevik power. Moreover, it was constrained by the Anglo-Japanese Alliance to follow a more moderate and conciliatory course than the United States.

Informal Anglo-American negotiations reached agreement on several proposed changes in the Inter-Allied Agreement of 1919 on the Manchurian and Siberian railways. The Stevens Technical Board should be permitted to continue operation of the C.E.R., under the joint control of the interested powers including China, and financed by payment from the powers (such as France) in debt to the railway for past use of its facilities during the Siberian intervention.[48] Colby was confident that Japan would keep its as-

[46] Colby to Davis, August 5, and the Chargé in London to Colby, August 18, 1920, *For. Rel., 1920* **1**: pp. 704-705, 708-709. In subsequent exchanges the British and French governments sought to use the Russian gold in part payment of the Anglo-French loan to Russia, which matured on October 15, 1920. The American government objected that that would have the effect of making Great Britain and France preferred creditors, and again suggested using the funds for the C.E.R. (Davis to Wilson, September 28, 1920, Colby Papers).

[47] August 17, 1920, Daniels Diary.

[48] *For. Rel., 1920* **1**: p. 726; and *Papers Relating to the Foreign Relations of the United States, 1921* (2 v., Washington, 1936) **1**: pp. 564-566.

surances and eventually withdraw from Siberia, and he continued to seek Japanese cooperation in regard to the C.E.R.[49] In one of his last conversations with the British Ambassador on the subject, when Geddes indicated that Britain was cooperative but would leave the initiative to the United States, Colby warned that "we had taken the initiative already in making this proposal and that we wished to have frank understanding in the matter, and not expect the British to follow us and then look behind and not find them." [50] Geddes was advised that Great Britain should not try to assume the role of mediator between the United States and Japan, and that an Anglo-American common front would probably obtain speedy Japanese acceptance of the proposal. These problems remained unresolved when the Harding administration took office in March, 1921, but the State Department in the Colby era had begun to explore the essentials of a new Pacific system.

3.

The question of cable-landing rights on the Pacific island of Yap had first been raised by American spokesmen at the Paris Peace Conference. Lansing then suggested to the Council of Foreign Ministers the desirability of internationalizing Yap in the interests of world cable communications, and both he and Wilson had reserved the issue for further discussion.[51] Japan had occupied the former German island and included it among the territories for which it sought a mandate from the League of Nations. Yap's disposition was, of course, only part of the larger question of the disposal of the former German cables. It had been agreed at Paris that an International Conference

[49] S.D.File 861.00/6735, Archives.
[50] Memorandum of a conversation between Ambassador Geddes, Davis and Colby, February 24, 1921, S.D.File 861.77/2015, *ibid.*
[51] Extract from the minutes, April 30, 1919, S.D.File 862i.01/15, *ibid.*

on Communications should be held to discuss these and related problems, and with the authorization of Congress President Wilson announced that the conference would be held in Washington on November 15, 1920.[52] The State Department wanted a preliminary conference of the five principal Allied and Associated Powers to precede the formal meeting, in order to clear the way for a solution to the cables. At British request, that was scheduled for September 15.[53] Subsequently the Supreme Council at Paris decided that Yap should be held as a mandate by Japan, in accordance with the decision reached by the Council of Four on May 7, 1919.

The position of the United States at the preliminary meeting was that the peace conference had agreed that the cables were at the disposal of the five major powers, who collectively had an undisputed interest in them. Consequently, if final disposition of the cables could not be agreed upon, the American government would retract its previous consent to their operation on a temporary basis.[54] Obviously that position was intended to encourage an agreement, particularly in view of French and Japanese obstructionist tactics apparently designed to delay a final decision. The American and British delegates had already reached an amicable understanding on the Penzance-Halifax cable, but sharp differences had emerged with France and Japan over cables running between New York and Brest, Pernambuco and Monrovia, and the Pacific cable landing on Yap. In a broader sense, the American government was interested not merely in the ownership of the cables but in the prompt restoration of direct cable services between the United

[52] *For. Rel., 1920* 1: p. 116.
[53] *Ibid.* 1: pp. 116-117, 120, 125, 126. The Netherlands government expressed an interest in serving as the mandatory for Yap if the United States decided not to assume it (Memorandum of conversation with the Dutch counselor of legation, March 31, 1920, S.D.File 862i.01/8, Archives).
[54] Colby to the Chargé in London, November 4, 1920, *For. Rel., 1920* 1: pp. 135-137.

States and Germany as a matter of principle. In addition, as Colby noted, American public opinion was aroused and would be greatly angered if the Allies retained the seized cables: "not only would our part in the war bring us nothing under the treaty, but we would be distinctly injured by the action of our associates."[55] France was cautioned that it would be most serious if, as was rumored, its delegates left the preliminary conference in a week without coming to an agreement. The French delegates did not withdraw.

Colby's absence on his South American tour left the remaining negotiations in the hands of Norman Davis. Since it proved impossible to reach a decision on final disposition, a *modus vivendi* was concluded in mid-December, to last until February, 1921, for continued operation of the cables by the existing holders for the financial account of the five powers pending a negotiated settlement.[56] The formal conference on communications had to be postponed and became the responsibility of the next administration.

The issue over Yap also was unresolved. The American government maintained that it had lodged a specific reservation at the Paris Peace Conference in regard to Yap, separating it from the other Pacific islands to be granted Japan as a mandate. Lansing and Wilson had made reservations during discussions of the islands, and the State Department based its interpretation on the minutes of the Council of Four for April 21 and May 1, 1919. It was contended that when the President had agreed at the session on May 7 to grant the north Pacific islands as a mandate to Japan, his previous reservations in effect excluded Yap from the group. Therefore, the United States declined to acquiesce in the assignment of Yap to Japan.[57] The Allied Powers rejected the American contention, although the Ital-

[55] Colby to the Chargé in London, November 5, 1920, *ibid.* 1: pp. 137-138.
[56] *Ibid.* 1: pp. 147-148.
[57] *Ibid.* 1: pp. 263-264, 265-268.

ian government favored an attempt to reconcile the conflicting claims. Great Britain pointed out that since the League Council had already granted Yap as a class C mandate, the United States should discuss the problem directly with Japan. Norman Davis described the British comment as "flippant and unresponsive," "a complete disregard of our rights and contentions," and President Wilson agreed.[58] Apart from America's treaty rights, Davis pointed out, the League specifically had provided that the Allied and Associated Powers could designate the mandatories—yet Britain and the Allies had ignored the United States in determining the mandatory agreement. On February 21, 1921, Colby informed the League Council that the American government should be consulted prior to final action on proposed mandates, and that it could not acquiesce in the inclusion of Yap in the mandate to be granted Japan. The Council did delay approval of the mandates in Asia Minor and Central Africa, in accordance with Washington's request, but it had to reply that final action had already been taken in regard to the Pacific islands.[59] The controversy was not settled until after the Washington Arms Conference, when the United States and Japan signed a treaty in 1922 granting American citizens equal rights in the use of cables and wireless facilities on Yap and other Japanese mandated islands.

4.

Japanese-American relations were further irritated by continuing agitation within the United States for restrictive immigration and alien land laws. Advocates of Japanese exclusion and economically restrictive legislation directed at Oriental aliens in the United States had not been satisfied

[58] *Ibid.* 1: pp. 269-276; and Davis to Wilson, January 12, and Wilson's reply, January 13, 1921, Wilson Papers.
[59] *For. Rel., 1921* 1: pp. 89-92, 92-93.

by the Gentlemen's Agreement in 1907-1908 or by the 1913 California alien land law, and these people persistently sought adoption of more stringent measures. In April, 1916, Lansing had urged the Senate Committee on Foreign Relations to delete from an immigration bill a clause embodying the restrictive provisions of the Gentlemen's Agreement. The Japanese government wanted to avoid formal discriminatory restrictions, and Lansing assured the committee that Japan had faithfully observed the agreement. Although the House of Representatives had approved the bill with the objectionable provision, the Senate deleted it and a conference committee of the two houses concurred.[60] The State Department was also able to persuade the legislatures of Oregon and Idaho to abandon alien land measures aimed in effect at the Japanese.[61] After the United States entered the war, it seemed particularly desirable to the State Department to avoid affronting Japan by any kind of public debate or agitation of these problems. Therefore Lansing strongly advised a California congressman against arousing an impassioned debate by seeking repeal of the California alien land law at that time.[62] Later, from the peace conference at Paris, he cabled the California Senate that contemplated anti-Japanese legislation would be "particularly unfortunate." [63]

Anti-Japanese sentiment appeared to be more virulent after the war, stimulated by the excesses of wartime nationalism and patriotism. For example, the *Grizzly Bear Magazine*, published by the Native Sons of the Golden West, claimed in 1921 that the Japanese had a 100-year plan to acquire California and the Pacific West Coast for Japan. It seemed to many Americans living in the western

[60] April 24 and 25, 1916, Lansing Desk Diary; and April 25, 1916, and January 7, 1917, New York *Times*.
[61] February 3, 1917, New York *Times*.
[62] September 25, 1918, Lansing Desk Diary.
[63] April 11, 1919, New York *Times*.

states that the Gentlemen's Agreement was too porous, depending largely upon Japan to enforce its terms. So-called "picture brides" particularly aroused fears that the Japanese population in the United States was increasing at an alarming rate. The Gentlemen's Agreement excluded immigration of Japanese women of the laboring classes except for the wives of immigrant workers already in the United States. Picture brides were erroneously believed to be marriages arranged by proxy in Japan, whereby a Japanese woman could secure admission to the United States as the wife of an alien in America who had never seen more than a photograph of the woman before. Actually, under Japanese law, a valid marriage could be contracted not by a proxy ceremony but only by the deposit of an affidavit by both parties in a Japanese registry office.[64] Senator James D. Phelan of California introduced an amendment to an immigration bill that would have absolutely prohibited entry into the United States of Japanese immigrants of the working class, thereby substituting an act of Congress for the Gentlemen's Agreement. Since Phelan was primarily concerned with the picture brides, the Department's Division of Far Eastern Affairs suggested that congressional action possibly could be avoided if the Japanese government voluntarily would promise to withhold such passports.[65]

Ambassador Morris in Tokyo reported increasing resentment and irritation at America by elements in the Japanese public, the result of the Shantung controversy and the proposed alien land laws: "It appears to me quite clear that the military party is using the United States as the future menace, not sincerely but as a justification for in-

[64] *Papers Relating to the Foreign Relations of the United States, 1917* (Washington, 1926), pp. 849-872. The Department of Labor was dissuaded by the State Department in mid-1917 from ruling that the bridegroom would have to return to Japan to complete a fully legal marriage, and thus risking possible non-admission upon his attempted return to America.

[65] Memorandum, November 19, 1919, *For. Rel., 1919* **2**: pp. 415-416.

creased army and navy appropriations."[66] While he thought the situation not yet serious, it might become dangerous if a proposed anti-Japanese law were passed in California. The Foreign Minister, Viscount Yasuya Uchida, and Masanao Hanihara, the Vice Minister, expressed great concern to Morris and indicated a willingness to deny passports to picture brides.

Lansing discussed the problem with the Japanese Ambassador on November 20, 1919, and advised him that it would be politically wise for Japan to prevent abuses of the Gentlemen's Agreement. When the Ambassador inquired whether prohibition of picture brides would have a good effect on American opinion, he replied affirmatively.[67] Hanihara's assurances of tacit and effective action was welcomed by Lansing, but he pointed out that some more authoritative statement was desirable in order to satisfy critics in the United States and to preclude action at the next session of Congress. He left it to Morris to suggest to the Japanese authorities some acceptable device, which Lansing then could announce as proof that Japan had taken effective measures to perfect the Gentlemen's Agreement. The result was a Japanese announcement to the American government that measures had been adopted to prohibit picture brides from entering the United States.[68]

Far from subsiding after the picture bride issue apparently had been resolved, sentiment increased in California for a more stringent alien land law. An initiative measure was submitted to the California electorate in the fall election of 1920 to amend the 1913 act to prevent evasion of the prohibition against ownership of land for agricultural purposes by aliens ineligible for citizenship. The new measure would forbid the holding or leasing of land by

---

[66] Morris to Lansing, November 19, 1919, *ibid.* **2**: pp. 416-417.
[67] Memorandum, November 20, 1919, Lansing Papers.
[68] *For. Rel., 1919* **2**: pp. 417-419; and December 19, 1919, New York *Times*.

guardians, trustees, or holding companies acting for such aliens. As in the 1913 act, the phraseology of the amendment avoided specific reference to Japanese aliens, though it was designed to apply to them, and outwardly at least it seemed to be compatible with the naturalization laws and the Japanese-American Treaty of 1911. This was the situation, threatening indeed, as Colby took charge of the State Department.

Colby discussed the measure, then in petition form, at the meeting of the cabinet on May 25.[69] After it had been placed on the ballot, California's Governor William D. Stephens wrote to Colby in defense of the proposed initiative. Emphasizing the economic and social problems allegedly resulting from the growing Japanese population in that state (which contained approximately 80-85 percent of all the Japanese in the United States), the Governor attributed recent increases to evasions of the Gentlemen's Agreement. He thought the proposed law was certain to be adopted, and he urged the State Department to try to obtain stricter controls over immigration by negotiations with Japan. The only complete remedy, he concluded, would be exclusion by act of Congress, and he intended to recommend that to the California congressional delegation.[70]

Informal conversations between the Japanese Ambassador and the State Department began in the summer of 1920. During Colby's absence at the Democratic Convention, Ambassador Morris, called home for consultation, conferred with Ambassador Kijuro Shidehara about the proposed California initiative measure and related immigration problems. Upon his return to Washington, Colby declined to comment on the discussions,[71] delicate in re-

---

[69] *For. Rel., 1920* **3**: pp. 1-2.
[70] Stephens to Colby, June 19, 1920, *ibid.* **3**: pp. 2-11.
[71] July 14, 1920, New York *Times.*

gard both to Japan's sensitivities and the political situation within the United States. After a trip to San Francisco, Morris informed Shidehara that in his opinion the people of California were nearly unanimous in their determination to prevent Oriental immigration to the United States, a resolve based less on economic grounds and more on the fear that Orientals were unassimilable. Morris very frankly declared that the Gentlemen's Agreement had not worked satisfactorily in preventing immigration, and that total exclusion would encourage better treatment for the Japanese aliens already in California. He thought that the initiative proposal would be approved and that any interference by the federal executive would only accentuate racial antagonism in California. Yet Morris professed doubts about the constitutional validity of the measure. Therefore he suggested that Shidehara reflect on a possible procedure for immediately handling the issue, by awaiting a federal court test of the 1913 alien land law and meanwhile discussing desirable changes in the Gentlemen's Agreement to exclude completely all Japanese immigration. Such a solution would strengthen the Hara ministry in coping with Japanese public opinion and a way would be opened either to modify the 1913 act if it were upheld or, if invalidated, to substitute for it a revised Gentlemen's Agreement to prevent further action by California. Shidehara expressed agreement with Morris' view. Admitting that some of the loopholes that allowed continued immigration of workers could be closed, he stated a readiness to discuss revision of the Gentlemen's Agreement.[72]

It was one of the topics, together with other Far Eastern problems, that Colby examined with British Embassy officials on July 27.[73] He concluded that the procedure sug-

[72] Memorandum by Morris, July 22, 1920, *For. Rel., 1920* 3: pp. 12-14; and Hikomatsu Kamikawa, *Japan-American Relations in the Meiji-Taisho Era* (Tokyo, 1958), p. 416.
[73] July 28, 1920, New York *Times.*

gested by Morris to Shidehara was workable and he forwarded a copy to President Wilson for approval. Wilson pronounced it "sound to [the] point of obviousness," and requested an outline from Colby on desirable revisions of the Gentlemen's Agreement.[74] The Secretary suggested that, while awaiting court tests of the California laws, Morris should negotiate informally with Shidehara changes in the Gentlemen's Agreement to preclude additional Japanese immigration. Meanwhile, Colby personally would inform Governor Stephens that he had instituted informal negotiations to resolve the issue and hoped to protect California's interests while preserving friendly relations with Japan. Wilson apparently approved, for Colby wrote Stephens accordingly on August 28.[75] Colby also conferred with Shidehara, in the presence of Morris, and after reviewing the situation asked whether the Ambassador would request his government for an authorization with broad powers to negotiate a settlement with Morris.[76] After the interview, Colby informed newspaper reporters that he hoped the problem could be settled in a manner satisfactory to all concerned.[77] In early September, Governor Stephens called on Colby for a lengthy conference, after which each man spoke cordially of the other's cooperative attitude.[78]

The Japanese government agreed to the negotiations and made a successful effort to soothe Japanese opinion agitated by the proposed California law. The American Chargé in Tokyo reported that generally the Japanese press welcomed the efforts of the State Department to achieve a satisfactory solution, although opposition newspapers and chauvinistic organs took a critical approach.[79] Shidehara

[74] Colby to Wilson, August 18, 1920, Colby Papers; and Wilson to Colby, August 20, 1920, S.D.File 811.5294/92, Archives.
[75] Colby to Wilson, August 26, 1920, S.D.File 811.5294/104a, Archives.
[76] Memorandum by Colby, August 28, 1920, *For. Rel., 1920* **3**: pp. 14-15.
[77] August 29, 1920, New York *Times*.
[78] September 4, 1920, *ibid*.
[79] *For. Rel., 1920* **3**: pp. 15-16.

wanted Colby to issue a statement to allay Japanese resentment and fears, but the Secretary deemed it inadvisable in view of the domestic American political situation. The initiative seemed certain of approval, and the presidential candidates of the two major parties had endorsed California's course. He thought that nothing effective could be done to block passage of the act, and therefore that only a statement that the President viewed the measure as of doubtful legality and would prevent its enforcement would satisfy Japan.[80]

Increasing unrest in Japan, however, persuaded Colby and Undersecretary Davis that a general statement was necessary.[81] Drafted by Colby, a statement was released on November 1, the day before the California elections, that the State Department was studying closely the proposed California law and that no outcome in California would be acceptable to the entire country that did not accord with federal laws and the demands of justice.[82] The statement was reprinted in Japanese newspapers as evidence of the good faith of the American government. An apparently officially inspired story in *Asahi* also declared that the two governments had agreed on the basis of a new Gentlemen's Agreement, although some fears were expressed that the Republicans might impede that solution.[83] Even after the initiative measure had been overwhelmingly endorsed by the voters of California, the tone of the moderate and pro-government press in Japan, though expressing disappointment, sought to minimize that development and to anticipate the conclusion of a satisfactory agreement. Sensationalist and opposition journals, however, tried to exploit the deep resentment of the Japanese people and urged a resolute attitude toward the United States. The Chargé

[80] Colby to Wilson, October 4, 1920, Colby Papers.
[81] Davis to Wilson, October 30, 1920, S.D.File 811.5294/291, Archives.
[82] *For. Rel., 1920* **3**: p. 17.
[83] *Ibid.* **3**: pp. 17-18.

in Tokyo also again reported widespread apprehension in Japan that the incoming Republican administration would be more "imperialistic" and would encroach further on Japan in the future.[84]

Although Morris had reached an agreement in principle with Shidehara, nothing concrete could be achieved by Colby in the last months of an expiring administration. Morris wrote to Colby, before the presidential election, that he was preparing an agreement based on total exclusion of Japanese workers, with the United States reserving the right by act of Congress to put regulations into force against immigrants arriving in America; Japanese aliens in the United States were to possess by a treaty provision equal civil rights with other resident aliens, but not to include naturalization; the double allegiance of Japanese citizens in America would be abolished by a change in Japanese citizenship laws; and Japanese consuls in America were not to have jurisdiction over such persons.[85] After the election, Governor Stephens wrote Colby on two occasions that the new alien land law would be vigorously enforced and that California respectfully requested that treaty negotiations with Japan conform to the views of his state.[86] The Japanese Embassy and the State Department exchanged formal memoranda on the implications of the California law, while expressing confidence that the Morris-Shidehara conversations would be able to adjust the problem.[87]

Meanwhile, Senator Hiram Johnson of California launched an attack against the proposed revision of the Gentlemen's Agreement. Charging that the new agreement would not halt the influx of Japanese because control of

[84] Chargé Bell to Colby, November 5, 1920, *ibid.* **3**: pp. 18-19.
[85] Morris to Bell, October 29, 1920, *ibid.* **3**: p. 16.
[86] Stephens to Colby, November 15, and December 9, 1920, *ibid.* **3**: pp. 19-20, 20-21.
[87] *For. Rel., 1921* **2**: pp. 321-323.

immigration would be left to Japan, the Senator asserted that the new treaty would define the rights of Japanese aliens in America in a way designed to nullify California's alien land laws. Colby replied, not altogether candidly, that Johnson was poorly informed, and he promised to consult the Senate Committee on Foreign Relations about the provisions of a treaty or agreement before it was signed.[88] On the following day another heated press exchange occurred between Johnson and Colby. The Senator demanded that the public be informed of the tentative agreement reached by Morris and Shidehara. When Colby labeled as incorrect reports that such an agreement had been concluded, Johnson declared that "Either the press reports are erroneous or Mr. Colby is misinformed. I am constrained to believe that Mr. Colby is in error." Colby urbanely and smilingly commented, "If Senator Johnson wants to do the ghost dance on this subject, it must be without me as a partner." [89] The Secretary declined to send a copy of the Morris-Shidehara agreement to the Committee on Foreign Relations, pointing out that the terms were mere preliminaries and that publicity might defeat the desired end.[90] Even if an agreement could have been completed, the sentiment in California and the other western states and the imminent change of administration probably would have precluded its acceptance by the Senate. The problem was carried over into the Republican era and ended in total legal exclusion under the Immigration Act of 1924.

[88] January 30, 1921, New York *Times*.
[89] February 1, 1921, *ibid*.
[90] February 10 and 11, 1921, *ibid*.

IV. A New Era in Relations With Mexico

FOR A BRIEF PERIOD in 1920, it seemed that Mexican-American relations were on the threshold of a new era. Years of controversies and difficulties over the security of foreign lives and property in Mexico and the safety of the border regions apparently were over as a new regime took power in Mexico City prepared to seek friendship and cooperation with the United States. The high hopes proved premature, but at least the State Department under Colby's direction formulated the essentials of a satisfactory solution and marked the general directions that were to be followed to a successful conclusion by the Harding administration.

1.

Relations with the government of President Venustiano Carranza had been troubled ever since *de facto* diplomatic recognition had been extended by the United States in 1915. In addition to Carranza's inability to suppress the vestiges of revolutionary disorder, and thereby to protect foreign lives and property in Mexico, his plans for economic and social reform threatened the interests or enraged the sensibilities of influential groups within the United States. Many American Roman Catholics were disturbed by Carranza's anti-clerical policies, large landowners were alarmed at plans for land redistribution, and mining and oil companies were fearful that their holdings would be expropriated (American investments in Mexico in 1911 have been estimated as exceeding one billion dollars). Article 27 of the 1917 Mexican Constitution reserved ownership of all sub-surface mineral and oil deposits to the Mexican people. Numerous inquiries and protests by the State Department elicited assurances that the provisions of the new constitution would not be applied to oil holdings obtained prior to 1917, but these assurances proved to be unreliable. Moreover, during the period of American belligerency in World War I, Carranza had adopted a policy of strict and rather unfriendly neutrality toward the United States. After the armistice, these strained relations further deteriorated, to the point that war nearly resulted in 1919 over the Jenkins affair. William O. Jenkins, a consular agent at Pueblo, was kidnaped by anti-Carranza rebels on October 19, 1919, and briefly held for ransom. Subsequently, after release by his captors, the consular agent (who did not have diplomatic immunity) was arrested by local authorities on suspicion of collusion with the rebels. The resulting loud outcry in the American press and in Congress led to demands for armed intervention to protect the rights of Americans in Mexico and to end an intolerable situation of nearly continuous irritants and outrages that dated back to the beginning of the Mexican Revolution in 1911. Secretary of State Lansing adopted an increasingly peremptory attitude during the Jenkins crisis and war seemed imminent, until the Mexican government ordered the release of the consular agent.

Even after settlement of the Jenkins affair, relations continued to be strained with Mexico City. Despite earlier assurances, Carranza continued efforts to apply retroactively Article 27 of the 1917 Constitution, refusing to allow American oil companies to drill wells on their holdings unless they formally agreed to accept the new petroleum code in effect nationalizing oil lands acquired prior to 1917.

Lansing recommended to the President, on December 7, 1919, that relations should be severed with Carranza. Wilson instead had directed a continuation of negotiations with Mexico. In a letter to the President on December 19, drafted by Henry P. Fletcher, the Ambassador to Mexico who was then in Washington, Lansing reviewed the problem and concluded that the "limits of diplomatic pressure" had been reached; if the American government failed to adhere to its policy of defending validly acquired American property rights in Mexico and remained inactive, Carranza would have gained his point. In addition to the consequent loss of prestige, the United States would possibly suffer a reduction in its oil supplies. He warned that the Mexican President probably would "go up to the point of a definite break with this Government before abandoning the policy. . . ." [1]

Still failing to secure the desired response from the recuperating Wilson, Lansing in early 1920 again warned him of the seriousness of the situation: "Are you aware that our relations with Mexico have been for several months considerably strained. . . ?" [2] He proposed that Fletcher be returned to Mexico City for a final attempt at a solution, including arbitration of the question of the retroactivity of Article 27; if these efforts, coupled with a warning about an impending rupture, failed, diplomatic relations should be broken. Consuls would remain, and the break might check Carranza or even aid in his removal from power, thereby giving the State Department an opportunity to negotiate with a new government. Fletcher attributed all the difficulties to Carranza's personal hostility, and drew attention to the Mexican leader's so-called "Carranza Doctrine," intended to counter the Monroe Doctrine and aimed at elimination of foreign and especially

[1] Lansing to Wilson, December 19, 1919, S.D.File 812.6363/620, Archives.
[2] Lansing to Wilson, January 3, 1920, Wilson Papers.

American influence in Mexico, a Latin American understanding without the United States, and the seeking of treaty ties between Mexico and some strong non-American state to offset the United States.[3] Wilson still failed to act and Fletcher, despairing of a solution as long as Carranza remained in power, resigned his post on February 12, 1920.[4]

2.

In April, soon after Colby had succeeded Lansing, a revolt began against the inefficient Carranza led by Generals Álvaro Obregón, Adolfo de la Huerta, and Plutarco Elías Calles. Accusing Carranza of attempting to dictate the presidential succession, the generals took to the field. Obregón occupied Mexico City on May 8 and two weeks later Carranza was killed. A provisional government was established under de la Huerta; on September 5 Obregón was formally elected President and he took the oath of office of December 1, 1920. The State Department's desire for a new regime had been fulfilled and more promising negotiations were now possible.

Businessmen interested in Mexico, such as E. L. Doheny of the Tampico Oil Industries, Harold Walker of the Mexican Petroleum Company, Cornelius Kelly of Anaconda Copper, William Loeb, Jr., of the American Smelting and Refining Company, and others, called upon Secretary Colby and advised great caution in recognizing the new government.[5] Their warning probably was unnecessary, as the

---

[3] Fletcher to Lansing, January 17, 1920, S.D.File 711.12/256, Archives.
[4] Fletcher had wanted to resign in mid-1919 but had remained at Lansing's request until Polk returned from Paris; he resubmitted his resignation on January 20, 1920 (Lansing Papers).
[5] May 20, 1920, New York *Times*. In July, the former Secretary of the Interior, Franklin K. Lane, and his employer, E. L. Doheny, called on Colby to present their view of the proper treaty arrangement.

Department appreciated the advisability of negotiating an understanding on outstanding problems as a necessary precondition for diplomatic recognition.[6] Early in June, the American Chargé in Mexico City reported that in a recent friendly conversation with Obregón, the general had described Carranza's anti-American policy as "a great mistake." Obregón then had stated his support of Pan American unity and acceptance of United States leadership, and he indicated his readiness to negotiate an understanding with Washington on all major problems. In the words of the Chargé, the general apparently was ready to "play the game."[7] Since Obregón seemed well disposed, Norman Davis recommended that the State Department should indicate its receptivity to negotiations. Wilson was interested but deemed it best to postpone action until Colby returned from the San Francisco Democratic Convention.[8]

It is noteworthy that, unlike the 1913 period when Wilson had denied Victoriana Huerta recognition on moral and ideological grounds, no great emphasis was placed by the American policy makers on the fact that the de la Huerta-Obregón regime had come to power by violence and revolution or that President Carranza had been murdered in the process. Of course, the new rulers were to sanction their position by apparently free general elections, without which Wilson might have balked at recognition. Yet the prevailing tone within the American government in 1920 seemed to be one of relief at Carranza's overthrow and a resolve to settle outstanding issues with the more promising new gov-

---

[6] Colby to the Chargé in Mexico City, May 25, 1920, *For. Rel., 1920* **3**: p. 167. Colby and the State Department requested the Navy to send warships to Mexican waters in case of further disorder. Daniels concurred but advised the President against any public announcement of the move; Wilson approved. E. David Cronon, ed., *The Cabinet Diaries of Josephus Daniels, 1913-1921* (Lincoln, 1963), p. 525.

[7] Chargé George T. Summerlin to Charles M. Johnston, Chief of the Division of Mexican Affairs, June 9, 1920, S.D.File 711.12/531, Archives.

[8] Davis to Wilson, June 25, and Wilson's reply, June 26, 1920, Wilson Papers.

ernment. Idealism to a considerable extent had been supplanted by a more realistic approach.

Unofficial conversations between Davis and Fernando Iglesias Calderón, the would-be Ambassador of the de la Huerta-Obregón regime, failed to achieve an agreement but did explore fully the outstanding issues between the two countries. Davis initially expressed hope for a more favorable attitude by the new government and warned that such a development would be most opportune as "the unparalleled patience of the American people towards Mexico shows indications of exhaustion." [9] In subsequent conversations, Davis clearly implied that recognition would be extended only after definite arrangements, and not merely oral reassurances, had been obtained. In a second interview, Davis welcomed the new government's assurances about policy but commented that "it would be necessary for the present regime . . . to translate into actual performance some of the most important proposed rectifications." After the envoy stated that the new government would be willing to recognize valid property contracts made by previous Mexican regimes, and the settlement of any disputed claims by a mixed Mexican-American board, Davis commented again that recognition would depend upon the specific measures taken by the Mexican authorities.[10]

Further exchanges ensued with Iglesias Calderón after Colby's return from San Francisco. Undersecretary Davis brushed aside the Mexican envoy's argument that de la Huerta had merely succeeded to Carranza's office and insisted that, "There must be a reciprocal desire to enter into official relations, and such a desire must spring from a mutual appreciation of, and respect for, the inherent rights

[9] Memorandum of a Conversation with Fernando Iglesias Calderón, June 30, 1920, *For. Rel., 1920* 3: pp. 174-176. The conversation was in Spanish, as the envoy spoke no English and Davis dispensed with an interpreter.

[10] Memorandum, July 9, and Davis to Wilson, July 21, 1920, S.D.File 711.12/532, Archives.

of the citizens of one country when engaged in orderly and legitimate business enterprises within . . . the other." [11] Davis drew attention to reports indicating that the attitude of the new regime toward Article 27 and American interests seemed not to differ greatly from that of Carranza. He warned that continuation of the Carranza petroleum policies could only delay recognition. At the next interview, Iglesias Calderón declared that his government would not make Article 27 retroactive and that President de la Huerta was considering issuance of a decree revoking the acts of Carranza. Davis commented that subsequent presidential decrees could easily reverse such a declaration, and that some more effective method should be found to settle the issue conclusively and permanently. Presumably the Undersecretary meant that the Mexican authorities should not only conclude an arbitration settlement and make acts of restitution, but also should annul or revise Article 27 of the constitution. The envoy pled that his government necessarily was concerned with Mexican public opinion and politics, and he complained that he had been in Washington for two months without being able to present his letter of credentials to President Wilson. Unmoved, Davis replied that such a presentation might be interpreted as an indication of diplomatic recognition, to which American public opinion would be adverse unless the major problems had been resolved satisfactorily.[12] In mid-September, Iglesias Calderón, announcing that he would soon leave for home where he was to serve as a senator, informed the Undersecretary that President de la Huerta had sent him a telegram reiterating his desires for an adjustment and expressing the hope that Wilson would send a personal representative to Mexico City.[13]

The next stage involved a special mission by George

[11] Memorandum, August 24, 1920, *For. Rel., 1920* **3**: pp. 178-180.
[12] Memorandum, August 30, 1920, *ibid.* **3**: pp. 180-182.
[13] Memorandum, September 14, 1920, S.D.File 711.12/318, Archives.

Creel to Mexico. A progressive journalist and wartime director of the Committee on Public Information, Creel was an ardent defender of Wilson's idealistic course toward Mexico and hoped to facilitate a crowning success for that policy prior to the November elections in the United States. In his view, a settlement would be politically useful in the campaign, but if the effort were postponed until after the elections it might never by achieved. According to his own account, he saw the President in late September and, after an optimistic discussion of the problems, he was urged by Wilson to undertake a mission to Mexico to explore the possibilities of a solution.[14] Although Colby reportedly expressed doubts if de la Huerta would make the necessary concessions, he agreed to Creel's journey. Creel then left for Mexico, upon his own insistence and at his own expense, as a private writer. There he was convinced that the Provisional President and those around him were willing to reach a satisfactory agreement covering border clashes, payment of debts and claims owed foreigners, and pledges against confiscation of foreign-owned property. Creel returned to Washington in late October, accompanied by Roberto V. Pesqueira, the Mexican financial representative and de la Huerta's agent in the United States. Reporting to Colby and Davis, on October 23, Creel expressed complete confidence that the Mexican government intended to resolve the oil issue either by a presidential decree or by a Supreme Court ruling that Article 27 was not retroactive. Therefore he advised recognition and had drawn up an informal agreement as the basis for a protocol, a document that he reported Pesqueira was willing to sign. According to Creel, the Secretary of State reacted enthusiastically and praised his efforts as breaking "the stupid deadlock of diplomacy." [15]

[14] Creel to Colby (summarizing his role in the negotiations), October 23 and November 12, 1920, S.D.File 812.00/24746 1/2, 24774 1/2, Archives.
[15] *Ibid.*

Colby left the burden of conducting all the conversations with the Mexican agents to Undersecretary Davis. He hoped thereby to maintain a posture of official reserve and to permit a greater informality and flexibility in the exchanges. Davis had conferred with Pesqueira, the financial representative of the Provisional President, on September 23, prior to Creel's trip to Mexico City.[16] Pesqueira had outlined Obregón's efforts to establish closer relations with the United States. He commented that he personally had conferred with various oil company representatives in New York City in several unsuccessful efforts to discover their precise contentions. Unfortunately, he had found that the oil spokesmen were only interested in berating past Mexican acts and in threatening that diplomatic recognition would not be extended until their interests were satisfied. Davis replied that American policy was not controlled by the oil interests nor did the government seek to dictate terms for the establishment of formal diplomatic relations. Instead, he attempted to make a distinction between demands and conditions, declaring that when recognition was extended it would be on the basis of general principles and after the Mexican government had adopted measures to remove obstacles to harmonious relations. Pesqueira spoke of possibly solving the oil controversy and other problems by an impartial study or arbitration of claims, and he urged that such a settlement, for obvious political reasons, be made with de la Huerta prior to Obregón's inauguration. De la Huerta would be freer to act than his successor, who could then "take office with a clean slate."[17] The Undersecretary repeated that the State Department was not trying to dictate specific terms and that it was within Mexico's power to create conditions conducive to recogni-

---

[16] Memorandum of a Conversation with Roberto V. Pesqueira, September 23, 1920, *For. Rel., 1920* **3**: 185-187.

[17] *Ibid.*

tion. His cautious words clearly implied that what had been discussed so far was inadequate as a solution and that more was required, presumably along the lines of the modification or clarification of Article 27 prior to recognition.

Colby approved Davis' demand for "convincing proof" from the Mexican authorities of a readiness to settle controversies before a renewal of official relations. He wrote Wilson, after referring to the recommendation of Henry Morgenthau (nominated but never confirmed as Ambassador to Mexico) for immediate recognition, that he hoped soon to discuss the situation with the President for much veiled strategy was involved, including propagandistic and oil industry pressures and other "like bedevilments." [18] Apparently Colby had in mind the opposition to recognition voiced by Senator Albert B. Fall and groups formed to protect the interests of American citizens in Mexico, especially the oil companies and their attorneys. He commented to Wilson that the Mexican agents indeed seemed to agree that a satisfactory settlement prior to recognition was necessary, but that so far they had not gone beyond the stage of mere talk. Therefore, Creel's proposal that a special trip to Mexico would be timely seemed promising to him.

President Wilson agreed that recognition should be withheld until Mexico acted upon Davis' suggestions to Pesqueira, although he stated his willingness to hold the question open if Colby found any conclusive reasons to the contrary.[19] That position was adhered to by Davis in a subsequent discussion with Iglesias Calderón, who had called at the department to make his farewells before

[18] Colby to Wilson, September 25, 1920, Wilson Papers.
[19] Wilson to Colby, September 27, 1920, *ibid*. The Fall Senate Sub-Committee's report in early 1920 had urged that recognition be made contingent upon Mexican acceptance of a number of conditions. See United States Senate, *Investigation of Mexican Affairs*, Senate Document No. 285, 66th Cong., 2d sess., pp. 3369-3373.

leaving for Mexico City. The United States, said Davis, had indicated certain measures that would eliminate the main obstacles to recognition; otherwise, "nothing would be gained by a renewal of official relations and an immediate renewal of controversies. . . ."[20] All of this caution on the part of the administration was indicative not of concern with the interests of oil or land speculators but of a determination to protect the legitmate property interests of American citizens in Mexico and to place Mexican-American relations on a reliable basis.

While Creel was in Mexico, Colby tried to quicken the informal negotiations. At a press conference, he remarked, confidentially and not for direct attribution, that the Mexican government could obtain recognition fairly easily if it would cease acting "skittish" and discuss the details of the more serious issues.[21] After Creel had returned from Mexico City in late October with his optimistic report, discussions were renewed with Pesqueira. Success seemed imminent. Pesqueira embodied the promises and assurances that Creel had obtained from de la Huerta and Obregón in a draft letter to Colby dated October 26.[22] In it Pesqueira professed to sum up Mexico's exact position, in the light of his informal exchanges with Davis. Law and order had been restored in Mexico and the new government, seeking a "firm and enduring friendship" with the United States, was prepared to observe fully its obligations under international law and practice. A joint Mexican-American arbitration board should be established to adjudicate foreign claims that could not be settled otherwise. As for Article 27, both President de la Huerta and President-elect Obregón had stated that Mexican laws were not retroactive and confiscatory, and that Article 27 would not be so interpreted;

[20] Memorandum, September 28, 1920, S.D.File 812.00/17396, Archives.
[21] Note, October 6, 1920, Colby Papers.
[22] Pesqueira to Colby, October 26, S.D.File 812.00/24701 1/2, Archives.

that was a "solemn pledge" backed by the honor of Mexico, and recognition was therefore requested.

Colby sent Pesqueira's draft to President Wilson along with a statement that the Secretary proposed to release to the press simultaneously with the letter. Both Colby and Davis agreed that "the material conditions on which we have a right to insist" were embodied in Pesqueira's letter and that the preliminary negotiations for recognition could proceed on that basis.[23] Wilson approved and the two documents were released to the press on October 29.[24] Pesqueira's letter offered to sign a protocol to arbitrate pecuniary claims and declared that Article 27 would not be interpreted retroactively. Colby's accompanying statement acknowledged that Mexico had indicated a "creditable sensitiveness" to its duties and described Pesqueira's letter as offering a basis on which the preliminaries for recognition could take place.

Colby's statement caught Washington and the nation by surprise, though the general reaction appeared favorable. It seemed that all that remained was to reduce the generalities of Pesqueira's letter to a formal protocol, which would then be followed by diplomatic recognition. Spokesmen for the groups with special interests in Mexico were not pleased by the news, however, and a flood of requests descended upon the State Department that the demands of these land and oil interests must be satisfied prior to recognition. A rueful Colby wrote the President that the latter's earlier warning about the complications of the problem had not been superfluous, for since the press announcement the department had been inundated by people trying to fathom the administration's policy or to propose onerous conditions for recognition. Doheny and the

---

[23] Colby to Wilson, October 28, 1920, S.D.File 812.00/24757A, *ibid.*
[24] October 30, 1920. New York *Times;* and *For. Rel., 1920* **3:** pp. 189-191, 192-193.

other oil interests had been particularly active, hoping to preserve the status quo in order to use recognition as a weapon to drive a bargain with the Mexican government on their claims. Colby tried to fend off these pressures, emphasizing that while recognition depended upon the Mexican authorities making certain prior assurances and provisions, the State Department would not attempt to impose specific conditions upon that government.[25]

3.

The promise of success quickly faded. Alarmed at the delay in the signing of a protocol between the two governments, Creel hurried to Washington for conferences with Colby on the fourth and fifth of November. He found Colby rather vague or uncommunicative about the next steps the Department planned to take. Creel attributed the delay to the influence of "selfish interests in the United States—rich, powerful and unscrupulous—who do not want the Mexican question settled." [26] In fact, however, the lack of progress resulted from the Department's receipt of reports indicating Mexican insincerity or duplicity in the negotiations. Charles M. Johnston, Chief of the Division of Mexican Affairs, advised Colby on November 9 to suspend negotiations with

---

[25] Colby to Wilson, November 6, 1920, Wilson Papers.

[26] Creel to Colby, November 12, 1920, S.D.File 812.00/24774 1/2, Archives. During his visit to Washington to defend his recommendations, Creel stayed at Colby's house in order to continue the arguments, which were so bitterly disappointing to him that he would have left Colby's home immediately except for the lateness of the hour. Much to his embarrassment, after he had left the next morning he had to return to reclaim a detachable dental bridge that he had left on the bedside table.—George Creel, *Rebel at Large* (New York, 1947), pp. 79-80. Also see Creel's *The People Next Door: An Interpretive History of Mexico & the Mexicans* (New York, 1926), pp. 357-358; and U.S. Senate, Committee on Public Lands and Surveys, *Hearing on Leases Upon Naval Reserves*, 68th Cong., 1st sess. (Washington, 1924), pp. 2123-2344. Colby professed an inability to understand Creel's anger and accusations (Colby to Wilson, November 20, 1920, Wilson Papers).

Pesqueira.[27] Recent information from the embassy in Mexico City indicated that the Mexican government had no intention of concluding a satisfactory adjustment. Johnston cited President de la Huerta's public statement on October 24 that all foreign oil interests in Mexico but two had acquiesced to the government's view about the public ownership of subsurface oil and mineral deposits. De la Huerta's assertion was manifestly untrue, Johnston pointed out, and it contradicted the provisions of Pesqueira's public letter. In addition, General Salvador Alvarado, the Mexican Secretary of the Treasury, obviously a key figure in any settlement, had remarked on the floor of the Chamber of Deputies on October 22, "I have always been a bolsheviki, am one now, and will always continue to be one." Finally, an intercepted circular from de la Huerta to all Mexican diplomatic missions in effect disavowed Pesqueira's negotiations. Subsequently the American Chargé in Mexico transmitted a report from a reliable source that President-elect Obregón had told a radical member of the Chamber of Deputies that although publicly he appeared to have adopted a new policy toward the United States it was merely a device to obtain diplomatic recognition. According to this source, Obregón concluded his remarks with the assurance that he was a radical and would solve the oil question radically.[28] Colby and the Department naturally were disturbed by these reports and were inclined to view skeptically further negotiations with Pesqueira.[29]

The result was a hardening of the American position. Colby wrote the bitterly disappointed Creel that it would

[27] Johnston to Colby, November 9, 1920, S.D.File 812.00/24765 1/2, Archives.
[28] Summerlin to Colby, November 18, 1920, S.D.File 812.00/24775, *ibid.*
[29] Colby to Summerlin, November 20, 1920, S.D.File 812.00/24776, *ibid.* Summerlin reported on November 30 that the story seemed accurate, though Obregón might have made his comment only for domestic political reasons.

be necessary to obtain an "unmistakable, even the written, approval" of Obregón to a settlement prior to recognition:

Protestations of good resolves are pleasant to receive and pleasant to acknowledge, but their significance arises entirely from the probability of their translation into acts, and is lost entirely if that prospect is either absent or not assured.[30]

Apparently in response to Creel's complaint that Pesqueira was leaving for home without any departmental response to his last overtures, Colby resolved on a final effort at clarifying the requirements for a settlement. In a letter to Pesqueira on November 25, that subsequently was released to the press, Colby expressed satisfaction with the assurances "unqualifiedly" given by the envoy and suggested that commissioners be designated to draft a treaty embodying the settlement.[31] In effect he called for a clause in the proposed treaty that Article 27 would never be applied retroactively. Despite press reports from Mexico City that Obregón would accept the proposal, nothing was to be achieved within the few months remaining to the Wilson administration. Obregón obviously was in a difficult situation, caught between highly nationalistic and anti-Yankee public sentiment within Mexico and the desires of Washington for explicit conditions prior to recognition. Moreover, the Mexican President apparently preferred to await the inauguration of the Harding administration before proceeding with the negotiations. Yet although their efforts were not crowned with success, Colby and Davis had explored the principal issues thoroughly and had indicated the general path to be continued by Secretary of State Charles Evans Hughes. Recognition was finally extended to the Obregón government during the negotiation of the Bucareli Agreement in August 1923.

[30] Creel to Colby, November 12, and Colby to Creel, November 17, 1920, S.D.File 812.00/24774 1/2, *ibid.*
[31] *For. Rel., 1920* **3**: pp. 195-196; and December 1, 1920, New York *Times.*

V. Retreat From Interventionism

A SIGNIFICANT CHANGE in attitude toward Latin America, particularly the Caribbean area, occurred during the last year of the Wilson administration.[1] No doubt it is true that a general reassessment of policy did not take place in 1920.[2] A close examination of that year does reveal, however, that the State Department was increasingly disturbed by criticism at home and in Latin America of the Caribbean interventions, and that the administration was sensitive to charges emphasizing the contradictions between military rule in Haiti and Santo Domingo and principles of national self-determination and democracy incessantly trum-

---

[1] This chapter is a revision and extension of my article, "Bainbridge Colby and the Good Neighbor Policy, 1920-1921," *Miss. Valley Hist. Rev.* **50** (1963): pp. 56-78. I thank the editor of the journal for permission to use it. Samuel Flagg Bemis, *The Latin American Policy of the United States* (New York, 1943), p. 119, views Wilson as the precursor of the Good Neighbor Policy but concludes that his idealistic words were offset by the record of armed interventions in the Caribbean; not until this "imperialism" was liquidated in the Republican and New Deal eras could the new course toward Latin America fully emerge. J. Fred Rippy, *The Caribbean Danger Zone* (New York, 1940), pp. 245-248, agrees. Graham H. Stuart, *Latin America and the United States* (New York, 1943), p. 3, is silent on the beginnings by Colby of withdrawal from Caribbean interventions. Lawrence F. Hill, *Diplomatic Relations between the United States and Brazil* (Durham, 1932), and Arthur P. Whitaker, *The United States and Argentina* (Cambridge, 1954), ignore Colby's goodwill tour in those two countries. Wilfrid H. Callcott, *The Caribbean Policy of the United States, 1890-1920* (Baltimore, 1942), pp. 488-495, and Dana G. Munro, *The United States and the Caribbean Area* (Boston, 1934), p. 133, put little emphasis on the Wilsonian beginnings of Caribbean withdrawal; in his latest volume, *Intervention and Dollar Diplomacy in the Caribbean, 1900-1921* (Princeton, 1964), pp. 321-325, Professor Munro gives this development more extensive treatment.

[2] Bryce Wood, *The Making of the Good Neighbor Policy* (New York, 1961), pp. 4-6.

peted during the recent war. Moreover, the defeat of Germany and the growing power of the United States in world affairs diminished or removed fears of possible foreign interventions in the area of the Panama Canal. Finally, painful experiences in Santo Domingo and Haiti hardly encouraged the assumption of new responsibilities. The result of these and other factors was that the Wilson administration took practical and symbolic actions in 1920-1921 which began to match more closely American deeds with its professed ideals in Latin America and thereby contributed significantly to the progress of Pan Americanism.

Colby had an important role in this progress. Although he lacked a detailed knowledge of Latin America, he did bring a fresh approach to his office. This was important, for Wilson's physical limitations and his trust in Colby gave the new Secretary primary responsibility for policy in Latin America. Although Lansing, Colby's predecessor, had been far from insensitive to Latin American reactions, he had been greatly concerned with American security in the area around the Panama Canal and had pursued policies which had made the Caribbean virtually a United States controlled lake. Coming to office in the more secure period after the Great War was over, Colby could perceive more readily the need for a greatly relaxed course in that area and for new efforts to cultivate Pan Americanism in Latin America. Postwar resignations in the State Department also brought in new personnel, such as Leo S. Rowe and Sumner Welles, well disposed toward improving the American image in the eyes of its neighbors to the south. Rowe, who had traveled and studied in Latin America, served as Chief of the Division of Latin American Affairs from October, 1919, to July, 1920, when he became Director General of the Pan American Union. Sumner Welles, after completing a tour of duty in Buenos Aires, served as Rowe's assistant and then as Chief of the Division after the latter's departure.[3] The initiation of policies looking forward to an early end of the interventions in Santo Domingo and Haiti originated with these new departmental officials. Colby adopted their recommendations and in addition contributed his own talents in a highly successful tour of South America.

1.

As the European war ended, American intervention in Haiti and the Dominican Republic became the target of increasing criticism and denunciation. Armed forces of the United States had occupied Haiti in 1915 and the Dominican Republic in 1916 primarily for benevolent reasons, to end nearly chronic disorder and to promote reforms conducive to constitutional stability and social progress, although security considerations also played some role. Working through the American admiral in command of the occupation, the State Department had obtained the election of a compliant government in Haiti and instituted reforms of the civil service, finances, the military organization, and the educational, sanitation, and transportation systems. In Santo Domingo, unfortunately, native politicians proved uncooperative and a formal military occupational regime was established, to undertake reforms similar to those in Haiti. Lacking experience in such neo-colonial ventures and distracted by the greater demands of the war in Europe, President Wilson and Secretary Lansing prior to 1919 failed to give close supervision to the intervention regimes. Consequently the real control tended to be in the hands of the senior American naval officer in the Dominican Republic and the marine commandant in Haiti.

Some abuses almost inevitably had occurred in both

---

[3] Dana G. Munro, after writing his *Five Republics of Central America* (New York, 1918), also joined the Division of Latin American Affairs.

countries under the intervention regimes. The press had been censored and American officials at times had acted arrogantly and tactlessly. In Haiti, where a façade of native government rendered control more difficult, some members of the occupying forces had manifested racial prejudice against the Negro and mulatto populations. General Smedley D. Butler, U.S.M.C., the first commanding officer of the Haitian gendarmie, later testified that "The Haitian people are divided into two classes; one class wears shoes and the other does not." As for the former, a small minority of the population, "Those that wear shoes I took as a joke. Without a sense of humor you could not live in Haiti among these people, among the shoe class."[4] Some 2,000 Haitian *cacos* or rebels had been killed by the American forces, whereas only seven marines and 27 gendarmes had been slain, yet most authorities concede that the atrocity stories were grossly exaggerated.[5] Until 1918 the majority of Haitians either were satisfied or acquiescent in the intervention, with most of the opposition emanating from the native officials and politicians whose ambitions and authority had been severely restricted. At first many Haitians had hoped that the establishment of the treaty regime—the 1915 treaty formalized the status of Haiti as an American protectorate—would be followed by fewer controls and the launching of a program of economic development. Disappointment in both these hopes and the enforcement of the corvee law or forced work on the roads resulted in growing opposition and the *caco* revolt.

Opponents in Haiti formed a "Patriotic Union" and mounted a blistering oral attack against the intervention.

[4] *Hearings on Haiti and Santo Domingo,* p. 517.
[5] L. L. Montague, *Haiti and the United States, 1714-1938* (Durham, 1940), pp. 233-236. See the account by a sociologist who studied the occupation regimes in the early 1920's, Carl Kelsey, "The American Intervention in Haiti and the Dominican Republic," *Annals Amer. Acad. Polit. and Soc. Science* **189** (1922): pp. 109-199.

Dominican discontent was also organized, and the protests of these two groups aroused sympathetic responses throughout Latin America and in the United States. Journals such as *The Nation* carried a number of critical editorials and articles condemning the occupation regimes as autocratic militaristic experiments unworthy of a democratic country and painting a disturbing picture of American brutalities in the island. Officials of the National Association for the Advancement of Colored People joined in the attack.[6] The issue also became involved in American politics when the Democratic vice-presidential nominee, Franklin D. Roosevelt, made a speech in Montana in August, 1920, in which he ridiculed Republican concern about the six votes of the British Empire in the League Assembly and declared that the United States because of its role in the Caribbean would benefit from about twelve votes in that body. In the course of his remarks, Roosevelt rather flippantly referred to his own role while in the Navy Department in drafting the 1918 Haitian constitution, designed to ensure continuance of American instituted reforms. Republicans mounted a sharp counterattack against the interventions and their presidential candidate, Warren G. Harding, declared that if elected he would not countenance such despotic behavior.[7]

Relations with the Dartiguenave regime in Haiti steadily deteriorated after the European war. President Sudre Dartiguenave, formerly cooperative, began to complain about the failures to achieve desired economic progress and of the controls exercised by American officials.[8] Complaints to Washington brought little change, although Lansing while at the Paris Peace Conference was sufficiently affected

[6] *The Nation* 110 (February 21, 1920): p. 226; 111 (July 7, August 28, September 11 and 25): pp. 64-65, 236-238, 265-267, 307-310, 345-347; and September 21, 1920, New York *Times*. See Munro, *Intervention and Dollar Diplomacy*, pp. 365-387, for a recent account of the intervention and Haitian discontent.
[7] Rippy, *Caribbean Danger Zone*, pp. 246-247.
[8] Munro, *Intervention and Dollar Diplomacy*, pp. 377-380.

that he began to contemplate converting the marine brigade into a legation guard (on the Nicaraguan model), leaving the gendarmie responsible for public order. American officials in Haiti opposed such a change, however, arguing that it would make it impossible to achieve their goals. Secretary Lansing accepted their advice and denied Haitian complaints of brutality and abuses of martial law. Failure to achieve the financial and reconstruction aims of the intervention, he declared to Haiti's Minister, were attributed by the American legation officials largely to the Haitian government, which had been "constantly obstructive." [9]

The American officials in Haiti found it increasingly difficult in 1920 to obtain cooperation from the Dartiguenave government, apparently emboldened by the approaching end of the Wilson administration and the growing criticism in Latin America and the United States of the intervention. Ignoring the agreement of August, 1918, Haitian officials proclaimed laws without securing the prior approval of the American legation officials. Some of these measures were clearly antithetical to occupation policies. One difficulty involved the recharter of the Banque Nationale, a French-founded bank in which the National City Bank arranged to buy the remaining French-held shares, a development welcomed by the State Department in order to remove or diminish foreign influence in the republic. The revised charter of the Banque Nationale, approved both by the Department and by the Haitian Minister of Finance, contained clauses designed to protect Haiti's interests. Incorporation of an additional clause restricting the importation of foreign currencies until the old Haitian paper money issue was retired caused the Haitian government to refuse to ratify the agreement on the grounds that it adversely affected the national interest. In addition to Haitian protests, the American Foreign Banking Corporation and the Royal Bank of Can-

[9] *For. Rel., 1919* **2**: pp. 316-331, 336-340.

ada charged that the provision would result in a National City Bank monopoly in Haiti.[10] Dartiguenave managed to withstand the pressures of the American legation officials, overruled by Washington, on this point.

The American authorities—the rather ineffective Minister Arthur Bailly-Blanchard, Financial Adviser John A. McIlhenny, and Marine Commandant Colonel John H. Russell—despaired of securing the fiscal reforms deemed necessary for the success of the intervention. McIlhenny reviewed for the State Department the difficulties with the Haitian government over the Banque recharter and stated his apprehension that the Royal Bank of Canada was maneuvering to purchase the French shares, awaiting the expiration of the National City Bank's option and aided by an anti-American legal adviser in Haiti, Louis Borno. McIlhenny described the Dartiguenave regime as so "definitely and strongly anti-American" that the Cabinet should be reorganized and the government "made to understand that it must cooperate with the occupation. . . ."[11] Without consulting the Department, the legation officials on August 5 suspended the salaries of the Haitian President, Cabinet, and Council of State until there should be an improvement in attitude—that is, compliance with the American demands. Haitian officials reacted strongly and charged attempts at dictation.[12]

Although McIlhenny subsequently testified to a congressional investigating committee that Lansing had suggested salary suspension when he had conferred with him in Washington early in 1920,[13] Colby and his advisers were surprised and disturbed by an action that might compel even further intervention in the Haitian government. The

[10] *Ibid.* **2**: pp. 816-820, 823-824.
[11] McIlhenny to the Division of Latin American Affairs, July 21, 1920, *ibid.* **2**: pp. 762-767.
[12] *Ibid.* **2**: pp. 768, 770-771.
[13] *Hearings on Haiti and Santo Domingo*, p. 1435.

Department agreed with the legation officials on the necessity for Haitian cooperation to obtain the goals of the intervention, but Secretary Colby was sympathetic with Dartiguenave's sensitivities and was inclined to continue efforts at persuasion rather than coercion. Since Minister Bailly-Blanchard bore the final responsibility for the salary suspension, Colby expressed surprise at his action and sharply reminded him to keep the Department more fully informed of his intentions: "The Department must insist that you take no further action which is likely to commit this Government or to prevent the Department from acting freely on its own judgment." [14] In subsequent instructions, Colby urged the Minister to rescind the salary suspension if it were not already in effect, in order to avoid the appearance of compulsion in persuading Haiti to cooperate. When Bailly-Blanchard failed to comply, pleading continued Haitian obduracy, Colby expressed regret while formally supporting the action.[15] He had no choice unless he was willing to destroy the influence of the Minister.

Colby and Navy Secretary Daniels were deeply concerned about the situation. It was discussed at the Cabinet meeting on August 10 when Daniels raised the question of the charges of brutality against the occupation forces.[16] Implementation of the American program through a proclamation of martial law was considered but was rejected for the time as it might force Dartiguenave and his Cabinet to resign. After several conferences between Daniels, Colby, and Davis, it was decided, at Daniels' suggestion, to send Rear Admiral Harry S. Knapp to Haiti on a mission of conciliation. Colby hoped thereby to avoid the necessity for government by martial law.[17] Colby analyzed the problem

[14] Colby to Bailly-Blanchard, August 6, 1920, *For. Rel., 1920* **2**: pp. 771-772.
[15] *Ibid.* **2**: pp. 772-782.
[16] August 10, 1920, Daniels Diary. See Munro, *Intervention and Dollar Diplomacy*, p. 383.
[17] August 25, 26, and 27, 1920, Daniels Diary.

for the President, with particular emphasis upon Haiti's passage of harmful laws without submission to the American legation. He advised that Admiral Thomas Snowden be relieved of responsibility for Haiti, as he was burdened with the Dominican command, to be replaced by Knapp in whose discretion and ability Colby had great confidence. Wilson concurred in Knapp's mission as a visiting military representative, but not as the President's personal agent lest it create the impression of conflict with the legation.[18] Neither he nor Colby had much confidence in Bailly-Blanchard, but it was decided to send the admiral on an informal basis.[19]

Knapp was cautioned by Colby that the State Department was "above all anxious to avoid the necessity of taking any action in Haiti which may ultimately lead to military intervention . . . in the Haitian Government." [20] In announcing the mission to Bailly-Blanchard, Colby expressed grave concern at the tension between the legation officials and Dartiguenave, while tactfully explaining Knapp's visit as merely an effort to secure a solution through the injection of a new personality. Daniels, more inclined than the State Department to repudiate the legation officials, recorded after an earlier conference with Knapp, "We must clean house and if anybody has been unwise or has done wrong, we must punish the wrong-doer." [21]

Admiral Knapp, formerly military governor of Santo

[18] Colby to Wilson, August 28, and Wilson to Colby, August 30, 1920, Wilson Papers.

[19] September 1, 1920, Daniels Diary; and Colby to Wilson, September 6, 1920, Colby Papers. Daniels told Colby that "I would regard a military gov't. as a tragedy." He later asserted that he had urged Lansing to withdraw the marines after the European armistice but that the State Department had not agreed and Wilson had been preoccupied with other problems (Daniels, *The Wilson Era: Years of Peace, 1910-1917* [Chapel Hill, 1944], p. 179).

[20] Colby to Knapp, September 8, 1920, *For. Rel., 1920* **2**: pp. 797-799.

[21] Colby to Wilson, September 6, 1920, Colby Papers; Colby to Bailly-Blanchard, September 8, 1920, *For. Rel., 1920* **2**: pp. 796-797; and August 28, 1920, Daniels Diary.

Domingo, handled his mission with finesse. He promptly obtained a promise from Dartiguenave to meet the American demands and had the salaries for July and August paid. Despite his skill and his consideration for Haitian sensibilities, however, he soon had to report that Dartiguenave had not acted as desired and that he agreed with Bailly-Blanchard that salaries should again be suspended. Davis, acting for Colby, quickly vetoed a long-term suspension regardless of provocation. Patience and pressure eventually achieved a measure of success, and the Haitian government agreed to submit proposed laws to the legation for approval in accordance with the 1918 agreement. Further intervention was thereby avoided.[22] Yet Knapp reported pessimistically upon his return to Washington that Dartiguenave was less friendly than before and the general climate for the achievement of intervention goals was poor.

While Knapp's mission was underway, Colby in a public statement on September 20 indicated that the administration was contemplating withdrawal from Haiti in the near future. He denied charges that the National City Bank controlled the revenues of Haiti and defended the intervention as undertaken for the unselfish purposes of maintaining order, reorganizing Haitian finances, and contributing to the welfare and progress of the Haitian people. Answering domestic and foreign criticism of the occupation, Colby declared, "This country is engaged in a task which has only a benevolent purpose. It is a task which was undertaken for the benefit of the Haitian people. . . . The work which the United States undertook to do is nearing completion and upon its completion this Government hopes to withdraw and leave the administration of the island to the unaided efforts of the Haitian people."[23] While he undoubtedly

[22] *For. Rel., 1920* **2:** pp. 808, 810, 811. See Munro, *Intervention and Dollar Diplomacy*, pp. 383-384.
[23] September 21, 1920, New York *Times*.

exaggerated the achievements of the intervention, he made it clear that the Wilson administration desired no further involvement and would prefer to liquidate the occupation as soon as its objectives were reasonably secured. His successors were not to complete the process, however, until 1934.

2.

Although American rule in the Dominican Republic was generally moderate and reasonable, Dominican discontent increased in 1919. Many Dominicans, previously cooperative in the expectation that the military government would be withdrawn after making reforms, were alienated by indications that such was not to be the case. This was particularly true after Knapp was succeeded in 1919 by Admiral Snowden as military governor. Snowden lacked the tact of his predecessor and made little effort to work with local leaders; instead, he publicly spoke of a prolonged occupation to achieve the ends of the intervention.[24]

Lansing became aware of the discontent and took measures in 1919 to reassert State Department control of the military government. The former chief executive, Francisco Henríquez y Carbajal, went to the Paris Peace Conference to plead his country's case before that body. At Lansing's advice, given through Herbert Stabler of the Latin American division, Henríquez y Carbajal left a memorandum with the American peace commission and journeyed to Washington for discussions with the State Department.[25] In the ensuing exchanges, in the late summer and early fall of 1919, the Dominican spokesman reviewed the causes of

[24] Sumner Welles, *Naboth's Vineyard: The Dominican Republic, 1844-1924* (2 v., New York, 1928) **2**: pp. 803-810, 818-824; Munro, *Intervention and Dollar Diplomacy*, pp. 320-321. Also see Joseph Robert Juárez, "United States Withdrawal from Santo Domingo," *Hispanic Amer. Hist. Rev.* **42** (1962): pp. 152-190.
[25] *For. Rel., 1919,* **2**: pp. 98-99, 106-107, 107-108.

unrest and recommended the restoration of civil government and civil rights by relieving the occupation forces of all police duties, the restoration of municipal police courts, and the appointment of a consultative commission of prominent Dominicans to draft basic laws under American supervision; these measures would be followed in orderly sequence by the election of municipal councils, provincial governors, legislature, and a president, and the evacuation of the occupying forces in planned stages. The military government, with a very different concept of Dominican readiness for self-government, was greatly disturbed by reports of the interviews with Henríquez y Carbajal.[26] Lansing and the Department shared the military governor's view that the occupation would have to continue for a long time to achieve the desired ends, but they were anxious that something be done to assuage the discontent and to secure local cooperation.[27] Minister William W. Russell also was called home for consultations in late 1919. Upon the Department's recommendation, Admiral Snowden in November appointed an advisory board or council of four prominent Dominicans to aid the occupation authorities.[28] The council did make a number of suggestions, most of which Snowden ignored, before its members resigned early in 1920 in protest against censorship of the press. After the wartime abdication of control, it was proving difficult for the State Department to reassert its proper authority.

In continuation of these efforts, the State Department under Colby proposed to the military government the creation of a new commission of prominent Dominicans to formulate essential laws on electoral procedures, education,

[26] *Ibid.* 2: pp. 120-121, 128-130.
[27] *Ibid.* 2: pp. 136-137. The Department considered but rejected plans to supplant immediately military rule by an American-headed civilian provisional government (S.D.File 389.00/2244, 2246, Archives).
[28] Phillips (for Lansing) to the American Minister, November 21, and Lansing to the Minister, December 10, 1919, S.D.File 839.00/2191a, Archives, and *For. Rel., 1919* 2: pp. 138-140, 145.

and sanitation.[29] Minister Russell, then in Washington, had recommended the measure which he and the Department hoped would have a beneficial effect in Santo Domingo and throughout Latin America. Admiral Snowden reacted adversely, however, pronouncing the proposed commission as not only useless in the present agitated state of affairs but likely to increase local agitation for an immediate American withdrawal. The military governor instead recommended a statement by the State Department that American control would be relinquished only when Dominicans could manage their own affairs competently, which recent events indicated was not yet at hand.[30] Snowden's quarterly report on April 1 had declared that it would require at least an additional ten years of control to establish a strong and honest Dominican government.[31] Apparently because of his opposition, the proposal for a commission was abandoned.

Continuing Dominican unrest caused the State Department to adopt meliorative measures. Dominican juntas had been organized to carry on anti-intervention agitation both within Santo Domingo and in Latin America, and a number of critical speeches were made and articles written during a patriotic week proclaimed in July, 1920.[32] Several individuals were arrested and tried for these activities, including the poet Fabio Fiallo who was fined $2,500 and sentenced to one year in prison. His case particularly aroused a storm of protest and sympathy in the United States and Latin America. Numerous telegrams of protest flowed into the State Department from Latin American press associations. Colby requested the Navy Department to have Snowden suspend the sentences recently meted to Fiallo and others,

---

[29] Polk (for Colby) to Chargé John Brewer, June 3, 1920, *For. Rel., 1920* **2**: pp. 110-111.

[30] Brewer to Colby, July 16, enclosing a memorandum from Snowden, dated June 29, 1920, *ibid.* **2**: pp. 115-120.

[31] *Ibid* **2**: pp. 111-115.

[32] Munro, *Intervention and Dollar Diplomacy*, p. 322.

which was done. To counter the criticism, the State Department also instructed its representatives in Latin America to release to the local press a general statement on the aims and achievements of the occupation.[33]

The problem of restoring and reorganizing the Dominican government had been considered within the State Department for some time. Various alternatives had been examined and rejected, but it was generally agreed that the military government must be ended.[34] Finally, Sumner Welles presented to the Secretary a memorandum that summed up the results of the deliberations within the Latin American Division. Withdrawal should take place in an orderly planned sequence. The first step would be an American announcement of its intention to return the government to the Dominican people; then a commission of Dominicans, aided by an American adviser, would be appointed to revise the laws and amend the constitution preparatory to self-rule; and all the recommendations of the commission would be subject to the approval of the military governor. Elections then would be held, the constitution amended, and self-rule restored. Only after these measures had been implemented and the Dominican government had accepted the goals of the intervention would the troops be withdrawn.[35] In forwarding the memorandum to President Wilson, Colby described Welles' recommendations as intended to answer criticism in Santo Domingo and to strengthen the American position in Latin America. He emphasized that the steps were merely preliminaries to a withdrawal which could not be completed until the purposes behind the intervention had been achieved. Wilson

[33] *For. Rel., 1920* **2**: pp. 132, 165-166.
[34] Memorandum by Stewart Johnson to Rowe, June 16, and a memorandum by W. W. Russell, June 23, 1920, S.D.File 839.00/2234, 2264, Archives. Welles' memorandum, below, followed the outlines of Johnson's recommendations.
[35] Undated Welles Memorandum, forwarded by Colby to the President on November 13, 1920, Wilson Papers.

approved the plan and authorized a public announcement of the intended withdrawal.[36]

Transmitting the draft proclamation to the President, Colby commented hopefully: "It marks the beginning of what I trust will be a steadily pursued and not protracted process of withdrawal from Santo Domingo." [37] In a letter to Secretary Daniels, for the guidance of Admiral Snowden, Colby explained that Dominican unrest and the adverse reaction of many Latin Americans had caused the State Department to give "thoughtful consideration to the question of whether the United States might now well take the first steps in returning to the Dominicans the Government of their Republic." Before withdrawal should be completed, arrangements would be made to continue "the essential measure of control" over Dominican finances through retention of the 1907 Convention.[38] Daniels apparently was in complete agreement, and the proclamation was issued by the military governor in Santo Domingo on December 23, 1920.[39]

The military government had not been consulted in this decision and, along with many officials in the Navy, it resented the State Department's brusque reassertion of control as premature and unwise.[40] The effect in Santo Domingo was also adverse—Dominican politicians and part of the press responded to the proclamation with a demand for an immediate restitution of sovereignty.[41] Yet a necessary beginning had been made and the State Department continued to curtail the authority of the military government. Undersecretary Davis requested that Snowden be instructed

[36] Colby to Wilson, November 13, and Wilson to Colby, November 15, 1920, ibid.
[37] Colby to Wilson, with enclosure, November 27, 1920, Colby Papers.
[38] Colby to Daniels, November 27, 1920, *For. Rel., 1920* **2**: pp. 136-138.
[39] December 1, 1920, Daniels Diary; and *For. Rel., 1920* **2**: p. 145n.
[40] *For. Rel., 1920* **2**: pp. 155-160. See Munro, *Intervention and Dollar Diplomacy*, p. 324; and Callcott, *Caribbean Policy of the United States*, pp. 487-489.
[41] *For. Rel., 1920* **2**: pp. 150-151.

to abolish the special provost courts and to rely instead upon the regular Dominican judiciary. He also asked that a decree curtailing freedom of the press and speech be rescinded and the sentences of several journalists canceled.[42] Snowden's plans for new long term public works, apparently based on the assumption that the occupation ought to last indefinitely, were rejected by the State Department. The admiral was reminded that the American government "has committed itself to initiate at once the preliminary steps looking toward a rapid withdrawal of its control in the Dominican Republic."[43] Davis, who had found it necessary earlier to emphasize to the Navy Department that the technical adviser to the proposed Dominican commission would represent the State Department rather than the military governor,[44] was convinced that the uncooperative admiral should be replaced. Aware of similar opinions held by other naval officers hostile to early withdrawal, Daniels defended Snowden as an honest and able if tactless administrator of the republic.[45] The admiral remained in charge, but the incoming Harding administration was to adhere to the intentions announced in 1920, though not to the plan adopted, completing the withdrawal of the marines in 1924.

Although Wilson wrote his son-in-law, William G. McAdoo, that "I don't care a damn what the Republicans do [about the Dominican question]. . . . There is nothing in it to be ashamed of at any point,"[46] the injection of the problem of Haiti and Santo Domingo into American domestic politics probably was a contributing factor to the decision to announce the preliminary steps to withdrawal.

[42] Davis to Daniels, December 13, 1920, *ibid.* 2: pp. 147-148.
[43] Davis to Daniels, January 7, 1921, *For. Rel., 1921* 1: pp. 854-856.
[44] Davis to Daniels, December 30, 1920, S.D.File 839.00/2291a, Archives.
[45] January 8 and 20, 1921, Daniels Diary. Knapp, thought of as a replacement by Davis, agreed with Snowden's views.
[46] Wilson to McAdoo, November 20, 1920, Papers of William G. McAdoo (Library of Congress, Manuscripts Division).

Yet as early as 1918, long before the political cross-currents of the 1920 presidential campaign, the State Department had become concerned about the Dominican military government and had begun to consider plans for a change in its form or name.[47] More basic to the decision to announce the intention of withdrawal, as Colby had emphasized, was the desire to assuage Dominican unrest and to answer mounting criticism in Latin America. Since Colby then planned a goodwill visit to South America, this factor was of immediate importance. With the war in Europe over, the State Department was less apprehensive that future disorders on the island might occasion embarrassing or dangerous European interventions. Finally, the decision to announce the intention to withdraw undoubtedly appealed to Wilson and Colby as a logical and inevitable step in accordance with American ideals and purposes.

3.

The 1916 Cuban elections had been attended by many charges of fraud. The Conservative candidate, Mario García Menocal, had been reelected President but the disgruntled Liberals had threatened revolution. The revolt failed after Secretary Lansing made it clear that the United States opposed revolutionary activities endangering the vital sugar crop. Both factions were then persuaded to accept the efforts of the American general, Enoch H. Crowder, in 1919, to improve the election laws.[48] As the 1920 elections approached, the State Department anticipated Liberal requests and strongly recommended to Menocal that Crowder should be invited to supervise the application of the revised laws in the election. The Cuban President, pleading

---

[47] See the previously cited memorandum by Stewart Johnson to Rowe, reviewing the problem, on June 16, 1920, S.D.File 839.00/2234, Archives.
[48] *For. Rel., 1919* **2**: pp. 8-9.

that Fernando Ortiz, a Liberal, was already publicly claiming that Crowder was to supervise the contest, declined to accept either supervision or observation by Crowder. He informed the American Minister, William E. Gonzales, that "he would retire from office before consenting to the humiliation . . . of supervision of elections." [49] The State Department abandoned its efforts and accepted Menocal's assurances that the election laws would be observed in full.[50]

Despite the reassurances, President Menocal subsequently alarmed the Liberals and disturbed the United States by planning changes in the Crowder laws. The threat of revolution again became imminent. Nevertheless, the State Department firmly resisted pressures to intervene. Before Colby took office, *ad interim* Secretary Polk in February, 1920, had refused to express an opinion about the nomination schemes of Menocal's Conservatives, though he opposed any alterations in the electoral code.[51] The new American Minister, Boaz W. Long, reported that Menocal planned to defeat the Liberal leader, José Miguel Gómez, by amending the laws to permit a Conservative fusion with a Liberal splinter group led by Alfredo Zayas. The existing laws prohibited such combinations, whereby a candidate's name appeared on more than one ticket, which constituted one of the forms of corrupt political bargaining used in the past. Colby continued Polk's policy of opposing legal changes, which nevertheless were made by Menocal.

[49] Phillips to Gonzales, October 23, and Gonzales to Lansing, November 7, 1919, *ibid.* **2**: pp. 77-79, 79-82. American electoral intervention in the Caribbean usually was interpreted locally as support for the party out of power and therefore often swung the victory to the outs. See the study by Theodore Paul Wright, Jr., *American Support of Free Elections Abroad* (Washington, 1964). For a more detailed account of the Cuban situation, consult George W. Baker, Jr., "The Wilson Administration and Cuba, 1913-1921," *Mid-America* **46** (1964): pp. 48-63; and Munro, *Intervention and Dollar Diplomacy*, pp. 503-518.
[50] *For. Rel., 1919* **2**: pp. 82-83.
[51] *Ibid.* **2**: pp. 1-3.

Desirous of avoiding further involvement in the election, Colby rebuffed Liberal overtures for a special conference in Washington: "Any attempt to transfer the forum of political activity . . . to Washington is harmful to the best interests of Cuba and is fruitful of endless misunderstandings." [52] The Department obviously was profiting from its past unpleasant experiences in Caribbean electoral controversies and apparently wanted stability in Cuba even at the cost of sacrificing genuinely free elections. Relying upon further reassurances from Menocal, the Department warned the Liberals not to boycott the election and rejected suggestions that it should supervise the balloting. Even if the Liberals did abstain, Colby made it clear that such a development would not prevent the United States from viewing the election as a valid expression of the national will. To hold Menocal to his pledges of a fair election, Colby pressured him into agreement to the issuance on August 29 of a public statement of his own promises of just procedures, followed on the next day by the release of an American statement of concern with the election.[53] As Colby had earlier written to President Wilson, he hoped in this manner to avoid electoral abuses and yet avert the necessity for direct intervention.[54]

Colby's optimism proved ill-founded. As the election approached, Undersecretary Davis became convinced that Menocal's promises and the American statement would not suffice to prevent disorders. He proposed, therefore, that General Crowder be returned to Cuba as Wilson's personal representative to emphasize that the United States was interested in a fair election, and to avoid the possibility of a later armed intervention to suppress revolutionary vi-

[52] Colby to Long, March 25, 1920, *For. Rel., 1920*, **2**: pp. 4-6.
[53] *Ibid.* **2**: pp. 9-14, 16-17, 19-20.
[54] Colby to Wilson, July 28, 1920, Colby Papers. Davis wanted to send Crowder *before* the election to try to avert abuses, but Colby apparently was opposed. See Munro, *Intervention and Dollar Diplomacy*, p. 511.

olence.[55] Wilson was inclined to agree and evidently Colby also concurred, for Minister Long discussed with President Menocal the proposed mission of Crowder as an observer at the elections. Menocal repeatedly interrupted Long's presentation with objections that the visitation would reflect adversely on his administration and would aid the Liberals. He refused to accept the proposal, therefore, although he indicated readiness to receive Crowder *after* the election. Faced with such stubborn resistance and anxious not to aggravate the situation, Wilson and Colby decided not to force the issue.[56]

In view of the threatened electoral disorders and probable revolutionary violence, Minister Long in October recommended that additional American marines be sent to Camaguey province to reinforce the small forces remaining there since 1917. American lives and property in the four eastern provinces of Cuba would be protected and a possible full-scale intervention avoided. Although the State Department initially was very reluctant to take such measures, Colby was finally convinced, only to have President Wilson refuse approval.[57] Davis' suggestion, at the request of Long, that warships be sent to Cienfuegos, Havana, and Santiago as a precautionary measure, was also rejected by Wilson. Davis argued that similar visits in the past had always had "a most quieting effect," but the President viewed the United States as authorized to intervene under the Platt Amendment only in cases of actual revolution and "not when we may fancy that revolution is impending."[58] Instead, Wilson favored a plan by Secretary of War

---

[55] Wilson to Colby, September 1, 1920, Colby Papers.

[56] Long to Colby, September 16, 1920, *For. Rel., 1920* **2**: pp. 21-22; and Colby to Wilson, September 18, and Wilson to Colby, September 20, 1920, Wilson Papers.

[57] *For. Rel., 1920* **2**: pp. 22-25, 27, 29.

[58] Davis to Wilson, October 16, and Wilson to Davis, October 18, 1920, Wilson Papers.

Baker to keep a division of American troops ready for possible intervention if the worst should occur.[59] Obviously, past experiences were making the President most cautious.

The November elections, as feared, were marked by violence and fraud. According to one historian, the party in power stole the election in an even more scandalous way than in 1916.[60] The defeated Liberals apparently planned to contest the results by appealing to the State Department. Still hoping to avoid intervention, Colby advised the Liberal leaders that they should exhaust the legal machinery in Cuba, for American action at that stage would be "an uncalled for and unwarranted intervention." [61] When it became obvious that the legal system was not functioning properly and that Cuba trembled on the brink of revolution, the State Department quickly decided to dispatch General Crowder to the island to resolve the crisis.[62] Menocal objected vigorously to the surprise visit and threatened not to receive the general, but the Department reminded him sharply of the right to intervene under the Platt Amendment: "on account of the special relations existing between Cuba and the United States it had not been customary, nor is it considered necessary, for the President of the United States to obtain prior consent of . . . Cuba to send a special representative to confer." [63] If Crowder's mission were successful, the Cuban President was to be informed, further American intervention could be avoided. Menocal had little choice but to capitulate and he agreed to receive Crowder. Wilson expressed pleasure that

---

[59] Wilson to Colby (enclosing Baker's note of the same day), October 16, 1920, Colby Papers.

[60] Charles E. Chapman, *A History of the Cuban Republic* (New York, 1927), pp. 399-400.

[61] Colby to Long, November 17, 1920, *For. Rel., 1920* **2**: pp. 40-41.

[62] *Ibid.* **2**: pp. 41-43.

[63] Davis to Long, January 4, 1921, *For. Rel., 1921* **1**: pp. 671-672.

Menocal had finally decided "to act like a gentleman." [64]

General Crowder did succeed in averting open revolution in Cuba. The courts were persuaded to quicken their reexamination of the disputed electoral returns. The general temporarily persuaded the rival factions to agree to a "pact of honor" but the Liberals subsequently broke it and used the traditional protest of the "outs" by boycotting the special elections. As the result, the Conservative candidate was certified victor and sworn in as the new chief executive. It was a victory for peace and stability, if not for democracy, and further American intervention, always a very real possibility, had been avoided. As Colby wrote in one of his last notes to Cuba, the only concern of the United States was that the elections should be honest, for only in that way would "the people of Cuba gain a respect for their own institutions and confidence in the processes of republican government." [65]

Another electoral problem confronted the State Department in Nicaragua. Here too every effort was made to avoid further intervention. In the Lansing era, the Department had expressed opposition to the plans of President Emiliano Chamorro to alter the constitution to permit his election to a second term.[66] Chamorro then selected his uncle, Diego Chamorro, as the Conservative candidate in the 1920 election. Some new officials in the State Department felt that the Chamorros represented a minority party apparently supported in power by the United States and advised supervision of the election to ensure a fairer result than in 1916.[67] Although their suggestion was not adopted, Colby proposed to President Chamorro that General Crowder

[64] Davis to Wilson, and Wilson to Davis, January 7, 1921, Wilson Papers.
[65] Colby to Crowder, February 21, 1921, *For. Rel., 1921* 1: pp. 676-677.
[66] Memorandum by Stabler of the Division of Latin American Affairs, August 5, 1919, *For. Rel., 1920* 3: pp. 292, 293.
[67] Munro, *Intervention and Dollar Diplomacy*, p. 418.

should be invited to Nicaragua to reform the completely inadequate election laws. Chamorro refused, claiming that the existing code was ample to ensure free elections. The American Minister, Benjamin L. Jefferson, feared that trouble would result if the election were not fair and he suggested that the Department should announce its expectation of free elections. A statement was issued to that effect.[68]

When violence occurred during voter registration at Managua and the government reportedly resorted to intimidation and force, Colby expressed to Chamorro the "deepest concern" of the American government and the "unfortunate impression" made on the American people.[69] A special American military attaché, Major Jesse I. Miller, was sent to the country and reported extensive padding of the registration lists and refusals to register opponents, and he warned that, since the election boards were controlled by the Conservatives, free elections could not take place.[70] Nevertheless Chamorro rejected all recommended safeguards and carried out elections marked by numerous frauds and acts of intimidation by the police and army. Only after his uncle was assured of election and of American recognition did President Chamorro agree to receive Crowder and to reform the electoral code for the next election.[71] The State Department had no alternative unless it withdrew the legation guard, thereby encouraging revolution and turmoil, or risked further intervention in Nicaraguan affairs. Obviously it was unwilling to do either and instead preferred stability with some promise of more democratic procedures in the future.[72]

Elections were also scheduled in Guatemala, where the

[68] *For. Rel., 1920* **3**: pp. 294-296.
[69] Colby to Jefferson, August, 1920, *ibid.* **3**: pp. 297-298.
[70] Miller to Colby, September 16, 1920, *ibid.* **3**: pp. 298-299.
[71] *Ibid.* **3**: pp. 300, 301-303, 306-313.
[72] See Munro, *Intervention and Dollar Diplomacy*, pp. 423-425.

brutal dictatorship under Manuel Estrada Cabrera was nearing an end. American diplomatic influence was restricted to requests that Estrada cease arrests and permit free procedures.[73] These efforts had begun under Lansing and Polk and were continued by Colby despite indications that Estrada would not observe his promises. Colby apparently regarded the reportedly senile dictator with some affection, later explaining to Wilson an intercession to obtain good treatment for him after his fall from power on the grounds that, though a despot, Estrada had been very loyal to the United States and its interests.[74] With adequate safeguards, Colby thought that it would be advantageous to Guatemala to allow Estrada to complete his term in office.[75] He flatly rejected repeated requests by the American Minister that American troops be dispatched to major Guatemalan ports. As he wrote the Minister, "Nothing short of the most serious menace to the lives of foreigners resident in Guatemala City would lead the Department to consider such a step. The mere fact of existence of disorder . . . would not justify so extreme a measure. . . . The Department deems it important to emphasize these fundamental principles of policy." [76] Estrada was later impeached and removed from office by the opposition on April 15. Grateful at escaping

---

[73] *For. Rel., 1920* **2**: pp. 720-723, 727-729.
[74] Colby to Wilson, November 18, 1920, Colby Papers.
[75] Colby to Minister Benton McMillin, April 1, 1920, *For. Rel., 1920* **2**: p. 737.
[76] Colby to McMillin, April 7, 1920, *ibid.* **2**: pp. 739-740. Lansing's general approach in the Caribbean had been sharply different. Thus on July 25, 1919, Lansing wrote Wilson that President Francisco Bertrand of Honduras was supporting his brother-in-law as his successor. The Department had protested that action as arbitrary but Bertrand rejected its advice and indicated a determination to perpetuate his family in power. Lansing advised that Bertrand and the opposition leader should be invited aboard the American cruiser *Denver* to confer and reach an agreement. If he did not, and turned to Mexico for support, "it may be necessary for the United States to proceed in a more forceful manner" to safeguard American lives and preserve the peace of Central America. Wilson concurred on September 1 that that course seemed to be the only solution (Wilson Papers). After further American pressure, including a threat to "consider actively assisting in the reestablishment of order and in overseeing the coming presidential elections," Bertrand abdicated and orderly elections were held. (*For. Rel., 1919* **2**: pp. 379-395).

a more serious crisis, the State Department extended recognition to the new government on July 21.[77]

4.

Colby's goodwill tour of South America climaxed his brief period in office. It originated in a rather haphazard manner. In the early months after the American entry into the war, the Brazilian Ambassador had discussed with President Wilson and the State Department the desirability of sending an American goodwill mission to his country.[78] About nine months later Lansing submitted to the President a memorandum from the Division of Latin American Affairs recommending a special mission to express American appreciation of the co-belligerency of Brazil and other Latin American partners in the Great Crusade. Wilson warmly endorsed the suggestion and requested the Secretary to consider the best plan and most available person for the tour.[79] Wartime exigencies, however, prevented action. At the Paris Peace Conference, Lansing approved the suggestion of Undersecretary Polk that Epitacio da Silva Pessôa, head of the Brazilian delegation to the conference and President-elect of his country, should be invited to visit the United States. It would strengthen relations with Brazil, he believed, and by acquainting Pessôa with the United States might offset his apparently friendlier attitude toward Great Britain and France. Wilson, through his private secretary, agreed.[80] By 1920, consequently, an obligation existed to return both Brazilian and Uruguayan official wartime visits.

---

[77] *For. Rel., 1920* **2**: p. 754. See George W. Baker, Jr., "The Woodrow Wilson Administration and Guatemalan Relations," *The Historian* **27** (1965): pp. 155-169.

[78] Memorandum by Stabler for Lansing, August 27, 1917, S.D.File 033.1132/2, Archives.

[79] Lansing to Wilson, May 15, and Wilson to Lansing, May 20, 1918, S.D.File 033.1132/5, 6, *ibid.*

[80] Lansing to Wilson, April 17, and reply, April 19, 1919, Wilson Papers.

Newton Baker, the Secretary of War, was aware of that obligation and in 1920 suggested that Latin America would appreciate a state tour by General John J. Pershing, the commander of the American Expeditionary Force to Europe.[81] Colby subsequently explained to President Wilson that Pershing "was something of a problem" after demobilization of the army and Secretary Baker was anxious to keep him "suitably and agreeably occupied." [82] With Wilson's approval, Colby informed the Brazilian and Uruguayan representatives of the proposed visit and received an at least outwardly favorable response.[83] Because of proximity and political importance, Argentina was then added to the itinerary.

After further reflection, and probably instructions from their governments, the Brazilian and Uruguayan Ambassadors in Washington decided that General Pershing was not entirely suitable for the proposed state visits. After the Brazilian Ambassador discreetly intimated his reservations to Colby, the department's Latin American experts discussed the tour with the diplomats involved and recommended that a visit by Secretary Colby would create a much more favorable impression.[84] It was pointed out that President Pessôa of Brazil headed the anti-militarist party in his country and that a roughly similar situation existed in Uruguay. In Argentina public opinion was very sensitive to alleged American resentment at Argentine neutrality in the war and might interpret a visit by General Pershing as a premeditated reflection or reminder. Furthermore, the opposition party, which had been pro-war, probably would

[81] Interview with Colby, June 19, 1930, Ray Stannard Baker Papers.
[82] Colby to Wilson, October 2, 1920, S.D.File 033.1132/102a, Archives; also in the Wilson Papers.
[83] Interview with Colby, June 19, 1930, R. S. Baker Papers; and Colby to the American Embassy at Rio de Janeiro, July 21, 1920, S.D.File 0.33.1132/6a, 9, Archives.
[84] Memorandum from the Division of Latin American Affairs to Colby, October 1, 1920, S.D.File 033.1132/12, Archives.

utilize the visit to launch a political attack upon the incumbents. As no prominent American official had visited South America since the highly successful tour of Secretary of State Root in 1906, Colby was urged to undertake the task.[85]

Colby laid the problem before President Wilson on October 2. He noted that both Dr. Rowe and Sumner Welles from the first had viewed Pershing as unsuitable, and that the Brazilian Ambassador "with much delicacy, but evident earnestness" had conveyed his objections. Since the Brazilian and Uruguayan visits to America had been largely inspired by respect and admiration for Wilson, if he could not go Colby's advisers recommended that a close representative be sent who could speak for Wilson's ideals and Pan Americanism in a way which a professional soldier could not: "A soldier hardly carries these connotations, and a uniform is not the garb in which South America finds the United States most ingratiating." [86] Undoubtedly the idea of the state tour appealed to Colby as a fitting climax to his secretaryship. His relations with Wilson were so warm and intimate, however, that he was genuinely reluctant to leave the side of the still impaired President: "I should hate to think that a moment might come when you needed me, or only wanted me, and I should not be here." [87] Yet Colby believed that the return of the visits of the Brazilian and Uruguayan chief executives should not be left to the next administration but should be made the final act of the Wilson administration. Wilson promptly replied that he too was distressed by the idea of a separation, but a visit by Colby would be "the ideal thing"; nothing should

---

[85] Secretary Philander C. Knox had visited Mexico and the Caribbean during the Taft administration, but his tactless remarks had increased rather than removed Latin American suspicions and resentments. See Callcott, *Caribbean Policy of the United States*, pp. 306-307.

[86] Colby to Wilson, October 2, 1920, S.D.File 033.1132/102a, Archives.

[87] *Ibid.*

be left undone to promote the goal of Pan American unity, "the only available offset to the follies of Europe." [88]

The itinerary was speedily completed, delayed only by difficulties with Argentina. Brazil and Uruguay promptly and warmly accepted the proposed state visit.[89] Trouble then ensued over protocol. Since Colby would be visiting Brazil and Uruguay on an official state visit as the representative of President Wilson but would come to Argentina only as a touring Secretary of State, the Argentine government, while expressing its pleasure, at first indicated that he would not be received officially as a "national guest." Ambassador Frederic J. Stimson reported, on December 1, that he had not yet been able to determine whether an official invitation would be issued to Colby or whether any preparations had been made for his reception and lodging: "As you are aware this Government has done that with nobody so far as I am informed, having a great desire for economy. . . ." [90] Apparently Argentine opinion was adverse to the visit, reflecting traditional rivalry with the United States and bitterness at the recent American tendency to condemn Argentine neutrality as pro-German.[91] The visit also was viewed as inopportune in view of its occurrence during the Christmas season. The State Department insisted that Colby be received as an honored national guest, and Ambassador Stimson was instructed to discuss the visit informally with President Hopólito Irigoyen to determine whether he would prefer its postponement to a more opportune time. It should be made clear, if Stimson saw Irigoyen, "that there does not exist now nor has there at any time . . . any trace of resentment because of the policy pursued by the Argentine Government during the war. Make clear likewise that the Secretary . . . does not intend

---

[88] Wilson to Colby, October 4, 1920, Wilson Papers.
[89] *For. Rel., 1920* **1**: pp. 228-230.
[90] Stimson to the State Department, November 29 and December 1, 1920, *ibid.* **1**: pp. 231-232; and S.D.File 033.1132/28, Archives.
[91] S.D.File 033.1132/28, 60, Archives.

in any way to refer to questions which have arisen during the past few years. . . ."[92] Although perhaps still unenthusiastic, the Argentine government officially invited Colby on December 22 to be the guest of the nation.[93] By then Colby had already sailed on his trip.

Colby's tour was intended as a major effort to reduce Latin American suspicions and to improve relations. Whereas an editorial in the New York *Tribune* declared that Colby should stay home as Latin America was in no mood to hear of cooperation and friendship in the light of the occupation of Haiti and Santo Domingo, the New York *Times* described the tour as one of the "most pretentious" moves since Root's visit, designed to launch a "new era" in Pan Americanism.[94] Time limitations caused Colby to restrict his tour to Brazil, Uruguay, and Argentina, despite overtures from Chile and other responsive countries. Another factor was Colby's sense of the dramatic, which convinced him that his trip would lose "something of distinctiveness and justification if I ramble around paying calls."[95]

Flying for the first time the specially designed flag of the Secretary of State, and accompanied by two reporters—William Crawford of the New York *Times* and Louis Siebold of the New York *World*—the Colby party was given a farewell send-off by the assembled Pan American diplomats and, to the salute of nineteen guns, sailed aboard the battleship U.S.S. *Florida* on December 4. Rear Admiral Frank B. Bassett and Major General Adelbert Cronkite accompanied the Secretary as aides. Off Cape Hatteras the battleship encountered heavy seas and a strong gale but the party

---

[92] Davis to Stimson, December 2, 1920, *For. Rel., 1920* 1: p. 232.
[93] Stimson to Colby, December 6, 1920, S.D.File 033.1132/38, Archives; Stimson to Davis, December 22, 1920, *For. Rel., 1920* 1: pp. 233-234; and December 25, 1920, New York *Times*.
[94] S.D.File 033.1132/60, Archives; and November 10 and December 6, 1920, New York *Times*.
[95] Colby to Wilson, November 27, 1920, Wilson Papers.

experienced no difficulty except for seasickness. After a brief stop at Barbados, the ship reached the waters off Rio de Janeiro on December 20.[96]

Brazil extended a cordial reception to Secretary Colby. He was escorted into the harbor of Rio de Janeiro by the cruiser *Rio Grande do Sul* and given a salute of nineteen guns; then the Secretary was visited by the Brazilian fleet admiral, the Foreign Minister, and Cabinet members before going ashore in the presidential launch to the Guanabara Palace, the former imperial residence provided for Colby's use. After luncheon, Colby paid a formal visit to President Pessôa, followed by an official dinner given in his honor by the President. Upon those occasions both men carefully avoided delicate topics such as the Monroe Doctrine and the League of Nations.[97] Colby was well aware of Latin American fears and suspicions. As the largest South American state, Brazil was apparently less concerned than others with the Monroe Doctrine and Caribbean intervention,[98] but like other staple-producing countries it was greatly dis-

[96] *For. Rel., 1920* 1: pp. 232-233; and November 25, and December 4, 6, 12, and 22, 1920, New York *Times*.

[97] December 22, 1920, New York *Times*. As an example of one of the problems the existence of the League of Nations offered to the Monroe Doctrine, Colby wrote Wilson on April 15, 1920, that Bolivia was insisting on carrying the Tacna-Arica boundary dispute with Chile to the League Council under Article 19 of the Covenant. Peru desired to do so also but would not act without the assent of the United States. Brazil, the only Latin American state then on the Council, was in a quandry and League officials feared that the United States would be irritated. Colby inquired whether Wilson viewed that development as a violation of America's "special interest in South America"; for himself, he did not see it as contrary to the Monroe Doctrine although he feared it would be misinterpreted by the American people and might have unfortunate repercussions on the question of membership in the League. Therefore he thought it advisable to intimate to the League that cognizance of the Bolivian request should not then be taken. Distressed because he wanted the League Council to demonstrate as soon as possible its peace-keeping role, Wilson concurred with Colby's view on postponement. So too did Senator Hitchcock when consulted (Colby to Wilson, April 15 and 30, and Wilson to Colby, April 16, and May 3, 1920, Wilson and Colby Papers). It was postponed until the Assembly session in 1921.

[98] See Clarence H. Haring, *South America Looks at the United States* (New York, 1929), p. 208.

turbed by the unfavorable postwar commodity exchange rates. In addressing the North American Chamber of Commerce in Brazil, Colby in effect denied charges that United States bankers had manipulated exchange rates to their own advantage and attributed fluctuations to the dislocations caused by the World War.[99]

In other addresses, Colby sought to create a favorable impression by reiterating Wilsonian ideals and defining the Monroe Doctrine as a benign hemispheric defense policy. He found his task greatly facilitated when he was introduced to the Brazilian Senate by Senator Alfredo Ellis who lauded the Monroe Doctrine as a United States assumption of the defense burden for the entire New World, defined by Wilson as a doctrine of defense only and not an excuse for control and exploitation.[100] Before the Chamber of Deputies, Colby declared that the Monroe Doctrine was a bond between nations dedicated to securing their independence and expressed the hope that it would never be used unfairly or become irksome. In bidding farewell after his brief visit, he reached new levels of eloquence:

> I had heard much of Brazilian hospitality, but it has surpassed all my expectations. . . . There is a strong bond between the United States and its sister republic of Brazil. . . . The roots lie in a similarity of our histories, in the logic of events, in the parallelism of our national aims and destinies. I leave Brazil with my heart overflowing with gratitude and kindliness, profoundly impressed with what the Brazilian nation has accomplished.[101]

The success of the Brazilian visit surpassed expectations. Brazilian officials and the press favorably compared Colby's tour to that of Root in 1906 and hailed it as a notable milestone toward a more vital Pan Americanism. The American Ambassador subsequently reported a universal feeling of satisfaction, expressed in such important news-

[99] December 24, 1920, New York *Times*.
[100] December 23, 1920, *ibid.*; and *For. Rel.*, *1920* 1: p. 234.
[101] December 25, 1920, New York *Times*.

papers as *O Paiz, Jornal do Brazil, Jornal do Commercio,* and others. An editorial in *O Paiz* expressed the general pleasure at the honor paid Brazil.[102]

Uruguay received the Secretary of State with even greater demonstrations of enthusiasm. Colby arrived at Montevideo on December 28 and found the city placarded with annoucements of his visit and in a gala Christmas mood. After reviewing an honor guard, Colby was given a parade through the city and a welcome by President Baltázar Brum. Entertainment was planned on a grand scale. Colby received the unprecedented honor of being the first foreigner and non-member to address a joint session of the Uruguayan Congress. In his reply to the introduction at the joint session, the Secretary voiced agreement with his introducer that the Monroe Doctrine was not meant to facilitate United States domination but was essentially a collective defense doctrine for all the hemisphere. Again, responding to a toast by President Brum, Colby congratulated Uruguay on its "national success and true greatness" and its vindication of the "hopes of democracy." He then defined the Monroe Doctrine as a "farsighted, unselfish, fraternal policy" and a "solemn affirmation by the United States of its belief in the capacity for self-government of each of the peoples of the Western Hemisphere."[103] Brum, who had visited President Wilson at the White House in August, 1918, and had long been a dedicated supporter of the Pan American cause, replied by praising the United States as a defender of liberty. The general Uruguayan attitude toward the United States reflected the twin facts that the country was one of the most progressive in Latin America and in a sense looked to the United States for diplomatic sympathy and support in its relations with its two large neighbors.[104]

The Uruguayan press also reacted with great warmth

---

[102] S.D.File 033.1132/77, Archives.
[103] December 29 and 30, 1920, New York *Times.*
[104] Haring, *South America Looks at the United States,* pp. 213-214.

and compared Colby's visit to the successful Root tour. In a "wildly applauded" farewell speech on December 31, the Secretary asserted that "It is our duty to find a way to allay this distrustful feeling [about the United States] and to exert every effort to wipe away any misunderstandings and merit your confidence. We ask to be judged by our merits and not by our defects." [105] Colby rightly attributed much of the genuine enthusiasm aroused by his tour to the ideals and labors of President Wilson. As he wrote Undersecretary Davis from Montevideo, "You can have no conception of the intelligent appreciation in South America of President Wilson and [the] unfeigned affections [in] which he is held. He would never believe it himself. My stay here has been touching in its cordiality." [106] The effect of the tour was manifested throughout Latin America. *El Mercurio* of Santiago, Chile, probably expressed the view of many observers when its editorialist commented on December 30 that while much of the importance of the tour would be lost because the incoming Harding administration would not accept or continue Wilsonian policies, it still was of continental interest as a manifestation of United States desires to strengthen interhemispheric relations.[107]

The Argentine reception was noticeably less enthusiastic. After an all night journey from Montevideo aboard an Argentine gunboat, the Secretary's party arrived in Buenos Aires on the morning of January 1. Only two or three hundred people greeted him, and they were mostly American citizens resident in Argentina, while the Argentine government was represented by an "Assistant Introducer of Ambassadors." [108] In part the nature of the reception undoubtedly could be attributed to the post-holiday exhaustion of the capital's residents and to a current chauffeurs' strike, but it probably also reflected the prev-

[105] January 2, 1921, New York *Times*.
[106] Colby to Davis, January 1, 1921, S.D.File 033.1132/62, Archives.
[107] Excerpt in the New York *Times*, January 1, 1921.
[108] January 2, 1921, *ibid*.

alent feeling of Yankeephobia. Argentines, as many other Latin Americans, tended to be highly critical of the American occupation of Haiti and Santo Domingo. Former Dominican President Henríquez y Carbajal was even then engaged in a propaganda tour of South America, during which he charged the United States with atrocities and undemocratic actions in Haiti and Santo Domingo.[109] He was in Buenos Aires just before Colby's arrival and contributed to the hostility toward the United States. In addition, as Colby had left on his trip, the American Senate disappointed many Latin Americans by again failing to approve the Colombian treaty making amends for the loss of Panama. Finally, many Argentines were also disturbed at the emergency tariff measure which had just secured the approval of the House of Representatives and would, if it became law, adversely affect Argentine exports to the United States.

Colby met the challenges successfully. After a cordial reception by President Irigoyen, whom he invited to visit the United States, Colby made a number of speeches designed to answer critics. He denied that American bankers were responsible for the unfavorable commodity exchange situation, pointed out that the tariff measure had not been adopted, predicted early ratification of the Colombian treaty, and reiterated his past definitions of the Monroe Doctrine as applying to Europe only and as a hemispheric defense doctrine. His remarks at the official banquet held in his honor were reported by Ambassador Stimson as "the most successful speech I have ever heard on a public occasion in Argentina." [110] It was an unusually frank address

---

[109] December 26, 28 and 29, 1920, *ibid*. On December 28, in Montevideo, Henríquez y Carbajal stated that he was pleased with the United States announcement on withdrawal and therefore would not try to discuss the question with Colby, but nevertheless would continue his Latin American mission.

[110] Stimson to Davis, January 3, 1921, *For. Rel., 1920* 1: pp. 234-235.

in which Colby admitted past differences with Argentina and urged as a remedy top-level conferences between responsible leaders of the two countries.[111]

Throughout his brief stay, Colby impressed Argentines with his considerable knowledge and great interest in Latin American affairs. The attitude of the Argentine press changed from initial hostility or indifference to nearly universal approval. An editorial in *La Nacion*, on January 1, expressed the widely felt satisfaction that Colby was one American who was well informed about South America. President Irigoyen personally returned Colby's official call and reflected the increasingly friendly atmosphere by remaining unusually long in conversation. When Colby departed on January 4, *La Epoca* summed up the altered mood: "Referring to the visit of Mr. Colby, there is only one thing to be regretted; its shortness." [112]

Colby returned to Washington in late January with every indication that his brief tour had been a triumph for the United States and Pan Americanism. He was greeted upon his return by the Chilean Ambassador, Beltram Mathieu, in behalf of the Pan American diplomatic corps: "But you have not only spoken, Mr. Secretary, but you have also listened. You have heard with the meditative attention of a student and with the sincerity of a high-minded statesman." [113] Colby was greatly pleased with his trip and he was determined to continue with greater efforts at hemispheric cooperation and friendship.[114] He told a meeting of the Cabinet that South Americans felt that the United States had not been helpful or cordial in the past.[115] While in Uruguay he had suggested a cultural exchange of pro-

---

[111] January 4, 1921, New York *Times*.
[112] American Embassy (Argentina) to the State Department, January 18, 1921, enclosing translated press articles, S.D.File 033.1132/94, Archives.
[113] February 3, 1921, New York *Times*.
[114] January 27, 1921, *ibid*.
[115] February 1, 1921, Daniels Diary.

fessors and students between universities in Latin America and the United States. Back in the United States, he advocated more study of Latin American history and languages, to correct "most of our assumptions" and to promote better hemispheric relations.[116]

The approaching inauguration of Harding tended to overshadow news of Colby's tour. The only extensive coverage of it was carried in the New York *Times* and the New York *World*. A New York *Herald* editorial, however, praised the Secretary's "lucid and graceful eloquence" on the trip. The New York *Times,* initially hostile to Colby's appointment, hailed him as "a very real, active and efficient Secretary of State." [117]

5.

As the Wilson administration drew to an end, members of the Cabinet discussed a farewell gift for the President. Daniels suggested, perhaps only in jest, that Colby call a special meeting without the President, to decide on a gift for him. Colby declined, quipping that "One Secy of State was bounced for calling a cabinet meeting—Did I [Daniels] want to get rid of him?" [118] Instead, the members decided on signing a joint letter of appreciation to Wilson, to be presented at the last session of the Cabinet. At the end of this final meeting, Colby spoke first and in a "graceful little speech" expressed pleasure at the honor of having served under Wilson and hoped for steady improvement in his health.[119]

Colby and Wilson for some time had been discussing

---

[116] February 20 and March 1, 1921, New York *Times.*

[117] S.D.File 033.1132/73a, Archives; and March 8, 1921, New York *Times.*

[118] February 21, 1921, Daniels Diary. Colby here referred to Wilson's charges that Lansing improperly had convened meetings of the Cabinet during his illness.

[119] Walworth, *Wilson* **2**: p. 408; Edith Bolling Wilson, *My Memoir* (Indianapolis, 1939), pp. 326-327; and Houston, *Eight Years* **2**: p. 149.

their future. Colby proposed a law partnership despite the retiring President's lack of experience: "You would be a great lawyer—indeed you are one now, because of your mind, your knowledge of life, of men, of great transactions, of the principles upon which human affairs are controlled . . . and the wide range and depth of your knowledge." [120] Colby promised to limit demands on Wilson's physical energies, for he would not need to observe regular office hours, his name would be especially valuable to the firm, and he could select the business which he cared to undertake. Thus appealed to and reassured, Wilson consented, to Colby's great joy. After the inauguration of Harding, the two men established offices in Washington and New York City; Wilson was admitted to practice before the bar in the District of Columbia by acclamation of the members, and in New York by a special act of the legislature.[121] The partnership lasted until January 1, 1923, when it was dissolved at Wilson's request because of his poor health and the restrictions he felt it necessary to impose upon the kinds of cases the firm could properly accept.

The remainder of Colby's career never quite reached the level of his earlier promise and his unquestioned talents. He served as a special assistant to the Attorney-General of the United States on enforcement of the anti-trust acts, in 1933-1934, but by 1934 joined such conservative Democrats as Alfred E. Smith, John J. Raskob, and John W. Davis in the American Liberty League in opposition to Franklin D. Roosevelt's New Deal. Colby felt it necessary to take a stand in defense of the personal and property rights of the individual, and of the duty of government to foster the private enterprise system against what he and others viewed as the collectivist trend of the New Deal. Therefore, he was highly critical of the Democratic presidential candidate in the 1936 election. Colby died on April 11, 1950.

[120] Colby to Wilson, February 22, 1921, Wilson Papers.
[121] Spargo, "Colby," p. 216.

The place of Colby among American Secretaries of State must necessarily remain a modest one. He was not in office long enough to leave a prominent record. Yet his relations with President Wilson, in contrast to both Bryan and Lansing, were so intimate and warm that he was able to establish an excellent working partnership with the chief executive. That fact, together with the greater freedom and responsibility for the Secretary resulting from the President's continued impairment, gave Colby at least one unusual opportunity for statesmanship despite the brief duration of his tenure. In Europe and the Far East the failure to ratify the Versailles Treaty restricted the American role to a peripheral and apparently ineffective one of opposing excessive reparations and unnecessarily harsh treatment of Germany, and attempts to curtail Japanese exploitation and expansion in Manchuria and Siberia. Yet in both these areas, the State Department under Colby's direction pointed the way to the course followed by the Republicans in the twenties: informal cooperation to restore a peaceful German economy, and cooperation with Great Britain to moderate Japanese behavior. Unfortunately the State Department under Colby did not have enough time or political support in Congress to resolve the immigration problem with Japan. Colby's most noteworthy act in regard to Europe, and that was largely negative, was to formulate explicitly for the first time the American policy of non-recognition of the Communist government in Russia. His most notable achievement, and one lost sight of by historians until recently, was in Latin America. He presided over and directed the beginning of the relaxation of American control or hegemony in the Caribbean, and he contributed significantly to Pan Americanism by culminating his secretaryship with an eminently rewarding and valuable if brief goodwill tour of South America.

VI. Wilson's Secretaries of State

DEAN ACHESON, a scholarly and reflective former Secretary of State in the Truman administration, has written that among the most important conditions for a Secretary's success are that he and the President must clearly realize who is President and who is Secretary of State. The Secretary of State should possess the confidence and respect of the chief executive if he is to be more than a diplomatic bureaucrat or figure head, and the President, though free to seek advice where he chooses, should accept his Secretary of State as his principal adviser and executive agent in foreign affairs. Appointment of a major political figure to the State Department with a following in his own right, perhaps even overshadowing the President politically, makes for a poor working arrangement. Finally, Acheson emphasized, "At the heart . . . of the conduct of our foreign relations . . . lies this primary task of understanding the forces at work, and devising, adopting, and energetically following courses of action to affect or meet these forces." [1] How well did Colby, in comparison with Bryan and Lansing, meet these criteria?

Bryan, alone of the three, came to the State Department as a major national political figure, three-times the presidential nominee of the Democratic Party and with a large and devoted following. Wilson reluctantly appointed him because it seemed advisable, as Colonel House put it, to

[1] Dean Acheson, "The President and the Secretary of State," in Don K. Price, ed., *The Secretary of State* (Englewood Cliffs, 1960), pp. 27-50.

have him where he could be watched closely and where his influence could be used in behalf of the administration. Contrary to Acheson's view, it probably proved to be a net gain, for Bryan worked hard for Wilson's domestic program and had a significant role in its success. One reason it turned out well, of course, was the intellectual and moral force of Wilson's personality which soon made him the unquestioned spokesman for his party and the nation. Moreover, Bryan understood his subordinate position and admired and loyally served the President. Yet it is possible that Bryan's sense of his own independent political position as a party leader strengthened his opposition to Wilson's neutrality policies in the spring and early summer of 1915, and it clearly helps explain his decision to resign and in effect appeal his case for peace to the American people. In that narrow sense it probably had been a mistake to appoint an influential politician to the State Department. Lansing was the only one of the three to be totally lacking in political stature, a key factor together with his previous experience as Counselor for the State Department underlying Wilson's decision to have him replace the Great Commoner. Colby fell in between these two extremes, a well-known political figure who, because of his independency, was without any sizable political following or backing. Perhaps in part for that reason, he proved most satisfactory to Wilson. Sensitive to political currents and a gifted platform speaker, Colby was able to expound policy effectively to the public without being tempted to an independent course.

Only Colby was able to establish a really satisfactory working relationship with President Wilson. The President simply could not respect Bryan intellectually, although he appreciated his moral fervor and courage. He came to view Bryan as an unnecessary burden in the conduct of foreign relations, especially during the neutrality era, and began to depend increasingly on his intimate adviser, Colonel House, and on departmental experts such as Lansing for the real work of foreign policy. Long before the Great Commoner resigned in protest, Wilson wished to be free of his presence in the Cabinet and he undoubtedly accepted his resignation with a great feeling of relief.

Lansing's relations with the chief executive initially were much better, for the President had acquired respect for his abilities and advice during the early months of neutrality. He valued the new Secretary, however, primarily as a technician in foreign affairs who was well acquainted with international law and the forms of diplomatic procedure and who could put the President's diplomatic papers in the proper form. He tended to think of Lansing, therefore, as a highly placed diplomatic clerk and apparently failed to perceive that foreign policy results from many lesser decisions and recommendations made on lower levels before rising to the top—in other words, he failed to appreciate that Lansing necessarily played a much larger policy role, through his recommendations, interpretations of international law, and the very manner in which problems were brought to the attention of the White House. Yet Lansing's influence would have been even greater if he had been able to establish a more intimate relationship with the President. This he was unable to achieve, in part because of his own reserve and critical judgment which prevented him from giving the kind of warm admiration and subordination that Wilson's temperament required. More importantly, their increasing divergence of views on the nature of the postwar settlement, especially the issue of collective security, caused Wilson to distrust Lansing, to view him as hopelessly conservative and reactionary, and finally even to disparage his very real abilities. Only the exigencies of events prevented Wilson from requesting Lansing's resignation long before February, 1920.

In contrast, Colby was able to manifest real affection and a genuine if flattering loyalty to the President. Wilson respected him morally and intellectually and relied upon him more than he had on his two predecessors. Because of fortuitous events, Colby was able to achieve something similar to Colonel House's special relationship with the President in the performance of his duties in the State Department. The State Department was able to function closer to the ideal and Colby served as a responsible administrator and principal adviser to the President on foreign affairs.

In many ways Lansing clearly eclipsed the other two Secretaries in knowledge of the thrust of world affairs and the nature of international relations. He was experienced, widely read and traveled, and had a good grasp of the national interests of other great powers. Some of his private memoranda notes in fact revealed remarkable perspicacity about present world realities and future tendencies. For these reasons he probably deserves to be ranked close to the top among American Secretaries of State since 1898. However, he lacked a certain kind of moral vision and imaginativeness in foreign affairs which, together with his impaired relations with President Wilson, kept him from the first rank. Bryan was almost totally lacking in an understanding of the world of diplomacy and international affairs, partially redeemed only by his unquestioned dedication to the cause of world peace. Also like Bryan, entering office inexperienced in diplomacy, Colby brought with him a strong measure of Wilsonian idealism and rapidly began to master the intricacies of his new position. Colby apparently was more sensitive than Lansing to the changed climate after World War I, particularly in the Caribbean and Latin America where he directed a statesmanlike endeavor to adjust American policies to a new situation.

None of these men can be dismissed as figurehead

Secretaries of State or merely administrators of foreign policy, not even Bryan and most certainly not Lansing. All three essayed the role of statesman to some degree, helping significantly to shape policy in various areas. Bryan's role was largest in the Caribbean and to a lesser degree in the Far East; Colby also in the Caribbean and in Latin America generally; while Lansing's contributions ranged from the Caribbean, to neutrality policies, intervention in the war, Russia, and the Far East. In the sheer bulk and importance of events and policy decisions, Lansing's secretaryship was unquestionably the most important. Yet the most promising secretaryship came at the end of the Wilson administration, too late to achieve very much. If Wilson had been fortunate enough to have had Colby lead the State Department from the beginning of his administration, executive harmony and efficiency would have been greatly improved at the very least. Significant new breakthroughs on important foreign policies would surely have been more possible and even probable than was to be the case.

Bibliography

(Most of these works have been cited in the footnotes, but some were used for background only.)

1. Manuscripts

Official:

Great Britain. Foreign Office Correspondence, 1920-1921 (Public Record Office).
United States Department of State. Diplomatic Correspondence, 1919-1921 (Foreign Affairs Section, National Archives).

Private Papers Consulted (in Manuscripts Division, Library of Congress, unless otherwise indicated):

Anderson, Chandler P.
Baker, Newton D.
Baker, Ray Stannard
Bryan, William Jennings
Burleson, Albert Sidney
Colby, Bainbridge
Daniels, Josephus
Davis, Norman H.
Hitchcock, Gilbert M.
House, Edward M. (Yale University Library)
Lansing, Robert
McAdoo, William Gibbs
Polk, Frank L. (Yale University Library)
Wilson, Woodrow

2. Printed Documents

Great Britain

The Parliamentary Debates. Fifth Series. House of Commons.
British and Foreign State Papers, 1914-1920. 1918-1923.
Documents on British Foreign Policy, 1919-1939. First Series, edited by E. L. Woodward and R. Butler. 1947-1958. (16 v., London).

United States

The Congressional Record.
Inquiry into Occupation and Administration of Haiti and Santo Domingo, Hearings pursuant to S. Res. 112, 67th Cong., 1st sess. 1921-1922. (2 v., Washington).
Papers Relating to the Foreign Relations of the United States, 1917, 1918, 1919, 1920, 1921, and Supplements. 1920-1936. (Washington).

Papers Relating to the Foreign Relations of the United States: The Lansing Papers, 1914-1920. 1940. (2 v., Washington).
Papers Relating to the Foreign Relations of the United States, 1919, The Paris Peace Conference. 1942-1947. (13 v., Washington).
Papers Relating to the Foreign Relations of the United States: Russia, 1919. 1937. (Washington).

3. Memoirs, Diaries and Journals

BAKER, RAY STANNARD. 1945. *American Chronicle: The Autobiography of Ray Stannard Baker* (New York).
COLBY, BAINBRIDGE. 1930. *The Close of Woodrow Wilson's Administration and the Final Years* (New York).
CREEL, GEORGE. 1947. *Rebel at Large* (New York).
DANIELS, JOSEPHUS. 1963. *The Cabinet Diaries of Josephus Daniels, 1913-21,* edited by E. David Cronon (Lincoln).
―――― 1944. *The Wilson Era: Years of Peace, 1910-1917* (Chapel Hill).
―――― 1946. *The Wilson Era: Years of War and After, 1917-1921* (Chapel Hill).
GRAYSON, CARY T. 1960. *Woodrow Wilson, An Intimate Memoir* (New York).
GREW, JOSEPH C. 1952. *Turbulent Era, A Diplomatic Record of Forty Years, 1904-1945* (2 v., Boston).
HOUSTON, DAVID F. 1926. *Eight Years with Wilson's Cabinet* (2 v., Garden City, New York).
LANSING, ROBERT. 1921. *The Peace Negotiations, A Personal Narrative* (Boston and New York).
LODGE, HENRY CABOT. 1925. *The Senate and the League of Nations* (New York).
MCADOO, WILLIAM GIBBS. 1931. *Crowded Years, the Reminiscences of William Gibbs McAdoo* (Boston and New York).
REDFIELD, WILLIAM C. 1924. *With Congress and Cabinet* (Garden City, New York).
TUMULTY, JOSEPH P. 1921. *Woodrow Wilson as I Know Him* (Garden City, New York).
WHITLOCK, BRAND. 1936. *The Letters and Journal of Brand Whitlock,* edited by Allan Nevins (2 v., New York).
WILSON, EDITH BOLLING. 1939. *My Memoir* (Indianapolis).

4. Books and Articles

ACHESON, DEAN. 1960. "The President and the Secretary of State," in Don K. Price, editor, *The Secretary of State* (The American Assembly—Englewood Cliffs), pp. 27-50.
ADLER, SELIG. 1957. *The Isolationist Impulse, Its Twentieth Century Reaction* (New York).
ALBRECHT-CARRIE, RENE. 1938. *Italy at the Paris Peace Conference* (New York).
BAGBY, WESLEY. 1955. "Woodrow Wilson, a Third Term, and the Solemn Referendum." *Amer. Hist. Rev.* **60**: pp. 567-575.
―――― 1962. *The Road to Normalcy: the Presidential Campaign and Election of 1920* (Baltimore).
BAILEY, THOMAS A. 1950. *America Faces Russia: Russian-American Relations From Early Times to Our Day* (Ithaca).
―――― 1944. *Woodrow Wilson and the Lost Peace* (New York).
―――― 1945. *Woodrow Wilson and the Great Betrayal* (New York).
BAKER, GEORGE W., JR. 1965. "The Woodrow Wilson Administration and Guatemalan Relations." *The Historian* **27**: pp. 155-169.

——— 1964. "The Wilson Administration and Cuba, 1913-1921." *Mid-America* **46**: pp. 48-63.
BAKER, RAY STANNARD. 1935-1939. *Woodrow Wilson: Life and Letters* (8 v., Garden City, New York).
——— 1922. *Woodrow Wilson and World Settlement* (3 v., Garden City, New York).
BEAVER, DANIEL R. 1966. *Newton D. Baker and the American War Effort, 1917-1919* (Lincoln, Nebr.).
BEERS, BURTON F. 1962. *Vain Endeavor, Robert Lansing's Attempts to End the American-Japanese Rivalry* (Durham).
BELL, H. C. F. 1945. *Woodrow Wilson and the People* (Garden City, New York).
BEMIS, SAMUEL FLAGG. 1943. *The Latin American Policy of the United States* (New York).
BLUM, JOHN M. 1951. *Joe Tumulty and the Wilson Era* (Boston).
BROWDER, ROBERT PAUL. 1953. *The Origins of Soviet-American Diplomacy* (Princeton).
BUEHRIG, EDWARD H., editor. 1957. *Wilson's Foreign Policy in Perspective* (Bloomington).
CALLCOTT, W. H. 1942. *The Caribbean Policy of the United States, 1890-1920* (Baltimore).
CHALLENER, RICHARD. 1961. "William Jennings Bryan, 1913-1915," in Norman A. Graebner, ed., *An Uncertain Tradition: American Secretaries of State in the Twentieth Century* (New York), pp. 79-100.
CHAPMAN, CHARLES E. 1927. "The Development of Intervention in Haiti." *Hispanic Amer. Hist. Rev.* **7**: pp. 299-319.
——— 1927. *A History of the Cuban Republic* (New York).
CLINE, HOWARD F. 1953. *The United States and Mexico* (Harvard).
COBEN, STANLEY. 1963. *A. Mitchell Palmer: Politician* (New York and London).
COLETTA, PAOLO E. 1964, 1969. *William Jennings Bryan* (3v., Lincoln, Nebr.).
CORWIN, EDWARD S. 1940. *The President, Office and Powers* (New York).
COX, I. J. 1927. *Nicaragua and the United States, 1909-1927* (Boston, World Peace Foundation) **10**: pp. 703-887.
CRAMER, C. H. 1961. *Newton D. Baker. A Biography* (Cleveland and New York).
CREEL, GEORGE. 1926. *The People Next Door: An Interpretive History of Mexico & the Mexicans* (New York).
——— 1920. *The War, the World and Wilson* (New York and London).
CURRY, ROY WATSON. 1957. *Woodrow Wilson and Far Eastern Policy, 1913-1921* (New York).
DANIELS, JONATHAN. 1954. *The End of Innocence* (Philadelphia and New York).
DE CONDE, ALEXANDER. 1962. *The American Secretary of State, An Interpretation* (New York).
DE NOVO, JOHN A. 1956. "The Movement for an Aggressive American Oil Policy Abroad, 1918-1920." *Amer. Hist. Rev.* **61**: pp. 854-876.
DUDDEN, ARTHUR P., editor. 1957. *Woodrow Wilson and the World of Today* (Philadelphia).
DUNN, F. S. 1933. *The Diplomatic Protection of Americans in Mexico* (New York).
FIELD, FREDERICK V. 1931. *American Participation in the China Consortium* (Chicago).
FIFIELD, R. H. 1952. *Woodrow Wilson and the Far East: the Diplomacy of the Shantung Question* (New York).
FIKE, CLAUDE E. 1962. "The United States and Russian Territorial Problems, 1917-1920." *The Historian* **22**: pp. 331-346.
FISHER, LOUIS. 1930. *The Soviets in World Affairs* (2 v., London and New York).

BIBLIOGRAPHY

GARRATY, JOHN A. 1956. *Woodrow Wilson, A Great Life in Brief* (New York).
GEORGE, A. L. & J. L. 1956. *Woodrow Wilson and Colonel House* (New York).
GERSON, LOUIS L. 1953. *Woodrow Wilson and the Rebirth of Poland, 1914-1920* (New Haven).
GRISWOLD, A. WHITNEY. 1938. *The Far Eastern Policy of the United States* (New York).
HACKETT, CHARLES W. 1926. *The Mexican Revolution and the United States, 1910-1926* (Boston, World Peace Foundation) **9**: pp. 339-446.
HARING, CLARENCE H. 1929. *South America Looks at the United States* (New York).
HILL, LAWRENCE F. 1932. *Diplomatic Relations Between the United States and Brazil* (Durham).
HOOVER, HERBERT. 1942. *America's First Crusade* (New York).
―― 1958. *The Ordeal of Woodrow Wilson* (New York).
ILCHMAN, WARREN FREDERICK. 1961. *Professional Diplomacy in the United States, 1779-1939* (Chicago).
JESSUP, PHILIP C. 1938. *Elihu Root* (2 v., New York).
JUAREZ, JOSEPH ROBERT. 1962. "United States Withdrawal From Santo Domingo." *Hispanic Amer. Hist. Rev.* **42**: pp. 152-190.
KAMIKAWA, HIKOMATSU. 1958. *Japan-American Relations in the Meiji-Taisho Era* (Tokyo).
KELSEY, CARL. 1922. "The American Intervention in Haiti and the Dominican Republic." *Annals Amer. Acad. Polit. and Soc. Science* **189**: pp. 109-199.
KENNAN, GEORGE F. 1960. *Russia and the West under Lenin and Stalin* (Boston and New York).
―― 1956, 1958. *Soviet-American Relations, 1917-1920* (2 v., Princeton).
KERNEY, JAMES. 1926. *The Political Education of Woodrow Wilson* (New York and London).
LA FARGUE, T. E. 1937. *China and the World War* (Stanford).
LASCH, CHRISTOPHER. 1962. "American Intervention in Siberia: A Reinterpretation." *Political Science Quart.* **77**: pp. 205-223.
LATHAM, EARL, editor. 1958. *The Philosophy and Policies of Woodrow Wilson* (Chicago).
LAWRENCE, DAVID. 1924. *The True Story of Woodrow Wilson* (New York).
LEDERER, IVO J. 1963. *Yugoslavia at the Paris Peace Conference* (New Haven and London).
LEVIN, N. GORDON, JR. 1968. *Woodrow Wilson and World Politics: America's Response to War and Revolution* (New York).
LI, TIEN-YI. 1952. *Woodrow Wilson's China Policy, 1913-1917* (New Haven).
LINK, ARTHUR S. 1957. *Wilson the Diplomatist, A Look at His Major Foreign Policies* (Baltimore).
―― 1954. *Woodrow Wilson and the Progressive Era, 1910-1917* (New York).
―― 1947. *Wilson: The Road to the White House* (Princeton).
―― 1956. *Wilson: The New Freedom* (Princeton).
―― 1960. *Wilson: The Struggle for Neutrality, 1914-1915* (Princeton).
―― 1964. *Wilson: Confusions and Crises, 1915-1916* (Princeton).
―― 1965. *Wilson: Campaigns for Progressivism and Peace, 1916-1917* (Princeton).
MAMATEY, VICTOR S. 1957. *The United States and East Central Europe, 1914-1918* (Princeton).
MARTIN, PERCY ALVIN. 1925. *Latin America and the War* (Baltimore).
MARX, RUDOLPH. 1960. *The Health of the Presidents* (New York).
MAYER, ARNO J. 1967. *Politics and Diplomacy of Peacemaking: Containment and Counterrevolution at Versailles, 1918-1919* (New York).
MILLSPAUGH, ARTHUR C. 1931. *Haiti Under American Control, 1915-1930* (Boston).

Montague, L. L. 1940. *Haiti and the United States, 1714-1938* (Durham).
Morley, James William. 1957. *The Japanese Thrust into Siberia, 1918* (New York).
Munro, Dana G. 1964. *Intervention and Dollar Diplomacy in the Caribbean, 1900-1921* (Princeton).
—— 1934. *The United States and the Caribbean Area* (Boston).
Notter, Harley. 1937. *The Origins of the Foreign Policy of Woodrow Wilson* (Baltimore).
Osgood, Robert Endicott. 1953. *Ideals and Self Interest in America's Foreign Relations* (Chicago).
Parkes, Henry Bamford. 1950. *A History of Mexico* (rev. ed., Boston).
Parks, E. Taylor. 1935. *Colombia and the United States, 1765-1934* (Durham).
Parrini, Carl P. 1969. *Heir to Empire: United States Economic Diplomacy, 1916-1923* (Pittsburgh).
Perkins, Dexter. 1941. *Hands Off, A History of the Monroe Doctrine* (Boston).
Pringle, Henry F. 1939. *The Life and Times of William Howard Taft* (2 v., New York and Toronto).
Radosh, Ronald. 1965. "John Spargo and Wilson's Russian Policy, 1920." *Jour. Amer. History* **52**: pp. 548-565.
Rippy, J. Fred. 1940. *The Caribbean Danger Zone* (New York).
Schuman, Frederick Lewis. 1928. *American Policy Toward Russia Since 1917* (New York).
Seymour, Charles. 1934. *American Diplomacy during the World War* (Baltimore).
—— 1926-1928. *The Intimate Papers of Colonel House* (4 v., Boston and New York).
—— 1921. *Woodrow Wilson and the World War* (New Haven).
Smith, Daniel M. 1963. "Bainbridge Colby and the Good Neighbor Policy, 1920-1921." *Miss. Valley Hist. Rev.* **50**: pp. 56-78.
—— 1961. "Robert Lansing, 1915-1920," in Norman A. Graebner, editor, *An Uncertain Tradition: American Secretaries of State in the Twentieth Century* (New York), pp. 101-127.
—— 1958. *Robert Lansing and American Neutrality, 1914-1917* (Berkeley).
—— 1959. "Robert Lansing and the Wilson Interregnum, 1919-1920." *The Historian* **21**: pp. 135-161.
Smith, Gene. 1965. *When the Cheering Stopped: the Last Years of Woodrow Wilson* (New York).
Spargo, John. 1929. "Bainbridge Colby," in S. F. Bemis, editor, *The American Secretaries of State and Their Diplomacy* (10 v., New York) **10**: pp. 179-218.
—— 1920. *Russia as an American Problem* (New York and London).
Spector, Davis Sherman. 1962. *Rumania at the Paris Peace Conference* (New York).
Strakhovsky, Leonid I. 1937. *The Origins of American Intervention in North Russia, 1918* (Princeton).
Stuart, Graham H. 1949. *The Department of State: A History of Its Organization, Procedure and Personnel* (New York).
—— 1943. *Latin America and the United States* (New York).
Tarulis, Albert N. 1965. *American-Baltic Relations, 1918-1922* (Washington).
Thompson, John M. 1966. *Russia, Bolshevism, and the Versailles Peace* (Princeton).
Tillman, Seth P. 1961. *Anglo-American Relations at the Paris Peace Conference of 1919* (Princeton).
Unterberger, Betty Miller. 1956. *America's Siberian Expedition: 1918-1920* (Durham).

WALWORTH, ARTHUR. 1958. *Woodrow Wilson* (2 v., New York).
WELLES, SUMNER. 1928. *Naboth's Vineyard: The Dominican Republic, 1844-1924* (2 v., New York).
WERNER, M. R. 1929. *Bryan* (New York).
WHITAKER, ARTHUR P. 1954. *The United States and Argentina* (Cambridge).
WHITE, WILLIAM ALLEN. 1924. *Woodrow Wilson: the Man, His Times, and His Task* (Boston and New York).
WILLIAMS, WILLIAM APPLEMAN. 1952. *American-Russian Relations, 1781-1947* (New York and Toronto).
WIMER, KURT. 1962. "Woodrow Wilson and a Third Nomination." *Pennsylvania History* **29**: pp. 193-211.
WOOD, BRYCE. 1961. *The Making of the Good Neighbor Policy* (New York).
WRIGHT, THEODORE PAUL, JR. 1964. *American Support of Free Elections Abroad* (Washington).
WRISTON, HENRY M. 1960. "The Secretary and the Management of the Department," in Don K. Price, editor, *The Secretary of State* (Englewood Cliffs), pp. 76-111.

Index

Aaland Island case, 43n
Acheson, Dean, 155, 156
Alexander, Joshua W., 58
Alien land law. See California, Japan
Allied Maritime Transport Council, 10
Allied Powers. See Great Britain, France
Alston, Sir Beilby F., 82-83
Alvarado, Salvador, 115
American Federation of Labor, 58
American Foreign Banking Corporation, 122
American Liberty League, 153
Anderson, Chandler P., 14n
Anderson, George W., 30
Anderson, Henry M., 14n
Anderson, William H., 13
Anglo-American Arbitration Treaty of 1911, 81
Anglo-Japanese Alliance, 80-85, 88
Anti-Saloon League of New York, 13
Argentina, 145; difficulties over Colby's visit, 144-145; neutrality, 142-143; receives Colby, 149-151
Armenia, 41, 42, 42n, 68
Armistice, 10, 34
Article 27 (Mexican Constitution). See Mexico
Asahi, 99
Asia Minor. See Turkey
Avezzano, Baron Camillo, 66

Bailly-Blanchard, Arthur, 123, 124, 126; Colby-Wilson lack of confidence in, 125
Baker, Newton D., 13, 13n, 30, 136-137, 142
Baker, Ray Stannard, on Colby, 20, 20n, 26
Baltic states, 61, 62, 66; also see Estonia, Latvia, and Lithuania
Banque Nationale (Haiti), 122-123
Bassett, Frank B., 145
Belgium, 76

Bemis, Samuel Flagg, 62
Benson, Admiral William S., 16
Bertrand, Francisco, 140n
Bliss, General Tasker H., 33, 35
Bolivia: Tacna-Arica dispute, 146n
Bolsheviks. See Russia
Borah, William E., 28, 28n
Borno, Louis, 123
Branting, Hjalmar, 74
Brazil, 145; origins of Colby's tour, 141, 142, 143; receives Colby, 144, 146-148; Tacna-Arica dispute, 146n
Brest-Litovsk (Treaty), 84
Brum, Baltázar, 148
Bryan, William Jennings, 1, 7, 26; Colby's views of, 15-16; at San Francisco convention, 26-27; compared with Colby and Lansing, 154, 155-157; cooling-off pact, 81; relations with Wilson, 2-4, 20n
Bucareli Agreement, 116
Bulgaria, 53
Burleson, Albert S., 22, 27
Butler, General Smedley D., 120

Cables (oceanic), 89-92
Caco revolt, 120
California alien land laws, 92-101
Calles, Plutarco Elías, 105
Caribbean. See Latin America, Haiti, Dominican Republic, Nicaragua, Guatemala
Carranza, Venustiano, 106, 108; "Carranza Doctrine," 104; Jenkins' Affair, 103; relations with United States, 102-103, 104-105
Casement, Roger, 16
Chamorro, Diego, 138, 139
Chamorro, Emiliano, 138-139
Chicherin, George, 70-71
Chile, 145, 146n, 149, 151
China, 76n, 82, 84; Consortium, 75-79; extraterritoriality, 71n; Manchurian railways, 79-80, 85-89

INDEX

Chinese Eastern Railway (Manchuria), 79-80, 85-89
Clemenceau, Georges, 17, 34, 35
Clemens, Samuel, 8
Comintern (Communist Third International), 67
Colby, Bainbridge, 33, 37, 51, 53, 91, 102, 105, 106; influence on policy, 1-2, 6; early career, 7-8; supports Wilson, 8-9; member of Shipping Board, 9-10, 16-17; appointed Secretary of State, 10-14, 14n; attitudes toward foreign policy before appointment, 14-18; administration of State Department, 18-19; and press, 19; promotes business abroad, 19-20; relations with Wilson, 1-2, 20-21; a third nomination for Wilson, 25-27; seeks approval of Versailles Treaty, 21-31; on Monroe Doctrine, 24-25, 146n, 147, 148, 150; election of 1920, 25-30; first League Assembly, 25n; R. S. Baker on, 20, 20n, 26; post-Versailles policy, 32; Ruhr crisis, 38-40; Armenian mandate, 40-41; Spa Conference, 42; Teschen dispute, 42-46; and Elihu Root, 43n; oil and mandates, 47-50; reparations, 54; non-recognition of Soviet Russia, 20-21, 55, 61-70; opposes Russian dismemberment, 61, 66, 67; trade with Russia, 57-60; Russo-Polish War, 61, 61n, 70; Spargo's influence on, 62, 64, 64n, Soviet reactions, 70-71; Polish expansionism, 72-74; Danzig crisis, 72-73; seeks positive Russian policy, 74; Far East, 75; Consortium, 78-79, 79n; opposes Anglo-Japanese alliance, 80-81, 82-84; advocates Anglo-American entente, 82-84, 89; and Irish-Americans, 15, 16, 83n; northern Sakhalin, 86-87; Chinese-Eastern Railway, 79-80, 85-89; cables and Yap, 90-91, 92; Japanese immigration, 96-101; clash with Hiram Johnson, 101; oil and Mexico, 105, 105n, 113-114; Carranza's fall, 106n; approves Creel mission to Mexico, 109, 111; Davis and Mexican negotiations, 110-111, 112; Pesqueira letter, 113; clash with Creel, 114-116, 114n; Mexican policy, 115-116; Pan-Americanism, 118-119; new approach to Haiti, 123-126; Dominican problems, 128-129; praises Welles' memorandum on Dominican withdrawal, 130-131; reasons for Dominican anouncement, 132-133; avoids intervention in Cuba, 134-138; Nicaraguan disorders, 138-139; Guatemala, 140-141; plans South American tour, 133, 141, 142-145; departs for South America, 145-146; Brazilian reception, 146-148; Tacna-Arica dispute, 146n; welcome to Uruguay, 148-149; successful Argentine tour, 149-151; pleased with goodwill tour, 151-152; final cabinet meeting, 152, 152n; law partnership with Wilson, 152-153; later career, 153; rank among Secretaries of State, 154; compared with Bryan and Lansing, 155-157
Colombia, 150
Committee on Foreign Relations (Senate), 101
Congress of Vienna, 17
Consortium (China), 75-79, 79n, 85, 88
Council of Ambassadors (Paris), 36, 38, 43, 45-46, 53-54, 72
Cox, James M., 27, 29
Crawford, William H., 29, 145
Creel, George, 108-109, 110, 112-113, 114-116, 114n
Cronkite, General Adelbert, 145
Crosby, Oscar T., 16
Crowder, General Enoch H.: Cuban electoral reforms, 133-134; mission to Cuba, 135n, 135-136, 137-138; and Nicaragua, 138, 139
Crowe, Sir Eyre, 83
Cuba, 133-134; Polk and Colby avoid intervention, 134-136; renewed disorders and Crowder mission, 136-138
Current Review, 7
Curzon, George Nathaniel, Earl of Keddleston, 41, 44-45, 48-50, 59-60, 70, 82n, 83n, 84-85, 86n
Curzon Line, 56, 65, 72, 74
Czechoslovakia, 42-46, 69-70

Daniels, Josephus, 21, 22, 30; at 1920 Democratic Convention, 27; Danzig crisis, 72; and overthrow of Carranza, 106n; Knapp mission to Haiti, 124, 125, 125n; Dominican withdrawal, 131, 132; farewell gift for Wilson, 152
Danzig, 72-73
Darmstadt, 39

INDEX

Dartiguenave, Sudre, 121-123, 124, 126
Davis, John W., 47, 48, 49n, 61n, 78n, 80, 81, 85, 153
Davis, Norman H., 22n, 23n, 42, 53-54, 70, 88n, 89n, 99, 109, 149; relations with Colby, 19; Versailles Treaty, 23; League Assembly, 25n; oil and mandates, 47, 50; trade with Soviet Russia, 60; and August 10 note to Italy, 65; Polish expansionism, 73; Chinese Eastern Railway, 80; Northern Sakhalin, 86; Russian gold, 88n; cables and Yap, 91-92; advises negotiations with Obregón, 106; conversations with Iglesias Calderón, 107-108, 107n; handles Mexican negotiations, 110-111; Dominican Republic, 131-132; Crowder Mission to Cuba, 135n, 135-136; advises force in Cuba, 136
Democratic Convention of 1920 (San Francisco), 25-27, 96, 106
Denman, Charles, 9
Denver, U.S.S. (Cruiser), 140n
Derby, Earl of, 44
Dodge, Cleveland H., 41
Doheny, E. L. (Tampico Oil Industries), 105, 105n, 113-114
Dominican Republic, 117, 118, 119, 125-126; reaction to U.S. intervention, 119, 121, 127, 150; Lansing considers changes in occupation, 127-128; advisory council ignored, 128; continued unrest, 129-130; Colby announces plan for withdrawal, 130-131; military government curbed, 132; Wilson defends policy, 132; withdrawal announcement, 132-133
Duncan, James, 64n

Ebert, Friedrich, 38
Elkus, Abram I., 43n
Ellis, Alfredo, 147
El Mercurio, 149
Estonia, 55-56, 69
Estrada Cabrera, Manuel, 140

Fall, Albert B., 111, 111n
Fiallo, Fabio, 129
Finland, 43n, 56, 67
Fiume. See Italy
Fletcher, Henry P., 104-105, 105n
Florida, U.S.S. (battleship), 145
Foch, Marshal Ferdinand, 39

Foster, John W., 1
France, 17, 123, 141; withdrawal of peace commission, 34-36; occupation of the Ruhr, 37-40; San Remo Conference, 40-41; and Wilson's suspicions, 33, 42, 51, 53-54; Teschen boundary dispute, 42-46; oil and mandates, 48-49; Fiume dispute, 51-53; trade with Soviet Russia, 57-58, 60; and Colby's note on non-recognition of Soviet Russia, 68, 69-70; Wrangel movement, 70n; Danzig crisis, 72; Consortium negotiations, 75-79 *passim*.; Chinese Eastern Railway, 86, 87, 88; Russian gold, 88n; cables, 90-92
Frankfurt, 38, 39, 40

Gade, John A., 64n, 65n
Geddes, Sir Auckland, 82, 82n, 86; Armenia, 41; Teschen dispute, 43-44, 45; Wilson's objections to, 47n; oil dispute, 48, 50; trade with Soviet Russia, 59-60, 70; Chinese Eastern Railway, 80, 87-89; and Anglo-American entente, 83-84, 89
Gentlemen's Agreement, 94, 95, 96, 97-101
Gerard, James W., 41
Germany, 3, 4, 5, 10, 15, 18, 28-29, 32, 33, 34, 35, 36, 42, 42n, 52, 53, 54, 62, 70n, 77, 89, 91, 118, 144; Ruhr occupation, 37-40
Gibson, Hugh, 45-46, 56, 61n, 73
Gómez, José Miguel, 134
Gompers, Samuel, 58
Gonzales, William E., 134
Grayson, Admiral Cary T., 13, 13n, 21
Great Britain, 15, 16, 17, 23, 32, 65, 74n, 141; withdrawal of American peace commission, 34, 35; Ruhr occupation, 37-40; San Remo Conference, 40-41; war debts, 42, 74n; Teschen dispute, 42-46; oil disputes, 46-50; Wilson's suspicions of, 42, 46, 51, 53-54; Fiume, 51-53; trade with Soviets, 57-60; reaction to Colby's non-recognition note, 70; Danzig, 72; and American cooperation in Far East, 75; Consortium, 75, 77, 78n, 79; Chinese Eastern Railway, 80, 85-89; renewal of Anglo-Japanese alliance, 80-85; Anglo-American entente, 82-84; Northern Sakhalin, 86, 87;

Russian gold, 88n; cables and Yap, 90-92
Grey, Sir Edward (Viscount of Fallodon), 78n
Grizzly Bear Magazine, 93
Guatemala, 139-141

Haiti, 117, 118, 119; reaction to intervention, 119-121; resistance to military government, 121-123, 150; U.S. announces withdrawal, 126-127
Hanihara, Masanao, 95
Hanna, Paul, 19n
Harding, Warren G. (and Harding Administration), 18, 25-26, 27, 28, 30, 54, 55, 69, 84, 89, 100, 102, 116, 121, 132, 152, 153
Hawkins, William W., 20n
Hearst, William Randolph, 8, 12
Henríquez y Carbajal, Francisco, 127-128, 150, 150n
Hitchcock, Gilbert M., 24, 146n; on Colby's appointment, 14, 22
Honduras, 140n
Hoover, Herbert, 22n
House, Edward M., 13n, 33, 47n; on Bryan, 3, 4, 155-156, 157; and Lansing, 5, 6; and Colby, 9-10, 16-17, 158
Houston, David F., 13, 13n
Huerta, Adolfo de la, 105, 107, 108, 109, 110, 112-113, 115
Huerta, Victoriano, 106
Hughes, Charles Evans, 8, 116
Hungary, 36
Huntington, U.S.S. (cruiser), 17
Hurley, E. N., 9

Iglesias Calderón, Fernando, 107-108, 107n, 111-112
Immigration Act of 1924, 101
Imperator, 14n
Inglaterra Mining Company, 14n
International Conference on Communications, 89-90
International Finance Conference, 42n
International Road Congress, 54
Irigoyen, Hipólito, 144, 150, 151
Irish-Americans and Colby, 15, 16, 83, 83n
"Irreconcilables," 36
Ishii, Kikujiro, 76n
Italy, 50, 64, 66, 70; Ruhr occupation, 39; San Remo Conference, 40-41;
Fiume dispute, 51-53; Yap issue, 91-92

Japan, 1, 32, 62, 75, 76n; Consortium, 75-79, 79n; Chinese Eastern Railway, 79-80, 85-89; Anglo-Japanese Alliance, 80-85; seizure of Northern Sakhalin, 86-87; Yap, 89-92; immigration problem, 92-101
Jefferson, Benjamin L., 139
Jenkins, William O., 103
Johnson, Hiram, 100-101
Johnson, Robert Underwood, 40-41, 41n
Johnson, Stewart, 130n, 133n
Johnston, Charles M., 114-115
Jornal do Brazil, 148
Jornal do Commercio, 148
Jusserand, Jules, 34, 37, 39, 70

Kelly, Cornelius (Anaconda Copper), 105
Kerner, Robert J., 69
Knapp, Admiral Harry S., 124-125, 127, 132n
Knox, Philander, C., 143n
Knox Resolution, 24, 24n
Kolchak, Admiral Alexander V., 63
Krassin, L. B., 58, 59, 60

La Epoca, 151
Lamont, T. W., 76-77
La Nacion, 151
Lane, Franklin K., 105n
Lansing-Ishii Agreement, 76, 77, 81
Lansing, Robert, 1, 2, 10, 11, 12, 18, 19, 20, 23, 51, 105, 105n, 152n; relations with Wilson, 4-6, 7, 20n; on Colby, 14n; withdraws peace commission, 33-37; oil rivalry with English, 47; Baltic policy, 55-56; nonrecognition of Soviet Russia, 55-56, 62; Polish expansionism, 56; Consortium, 75-78, 78n; Ishii, 76n; cables and Yap, 89-90, 91; Japanese immigration, 93, 94n, 95; Jenkins' affair, 103; advises break with Mexico, 104; and Latin America, 118; fails to supervise military interventions, 119, 125n; Haiti, 121-123; Dominican Republic, 127-128; Cuban disorders, 133; Nicaraguan elections, 138; Guatemala, 140; intervenes in Hon-

INDEX

duras, 140n; suggests goodwill tour of South America, 141; compared with Bryan and Colby, 154, 155-157
Latvia, 55-56, 69
League to Enforce Peace, 16
League of Nations, 2, 5, 16, 36, 39, 42n, 51, 55, 85, 89, 146; Colby endorses, 16, 17-18, 21-31; first Assembly session, 25n; mandates, 40-42; Aaland Island case, 43n; oil and mandates, 47-50; Yap, 89-90, 91-92; and Tacna-Arica, 146n
Lenin, Nicolai, 63, 70
Lithuania, 55-56, 61n, 69
Lloyd George, David, 52, 57, 74n
Lodge, Henry Cabot, 22, 24n, 31; and Colby's appointment, 12, 13-14
Lodge Reservations, 24n, 31
Loeb, William, Jr. (American Smelting and Refining Company), 105
Long, Boaz W., 134, 136
Long, Breckinridge, 18
Lusitania, 15

McAdoo, William G., 132
McCormick, Vance, 16
McIlhenny, John A., 123
McMillin, Benton, 140n
Manchuria. See China
Martens, Ludwig, 71, 71n
Mathieu, Beltram, 151
Menocal, Mario García, 133-138
Merle-Smith, V. S., 18-19
Mesopotamian mandate and oil, 20, 47-50
Mexico, 140n; Carranza regime, 102-103; Jenkins affair, 103; strained relations, 104-105; fall of Carranza, 105; Obregón-Huerta regime, 105-106; Davis-Iglesias Caldéron negotiations, 107-108; Creel mission, 108-109, 110, 112-113, 114-116; failure of attempts at settlement, 115-116
Miller, Jesse I., 139
Mongolia. See China
Monroe Doctrine, 23, 24-25; and "Carranza Doctrine," 104; Colby explains, 146-147, 148, 150; and Tacna-Arica dispute, 146n
Morgan, J. P. and Company, 76
Morris, Roland S., 79, 86; revision of Gentlemen's Agreement, 94-95, 96-98, 100, 101

Nation, The, 121
National Association for the Advancement of Colored People, 121
National City Bank of New York, 122, 123, 126
National Security League, 16
Native Sons of the Golden West, 93
Netherlands, 90n
New York *Globe*, 12
New York *Herald*, 152
New York State Committee on National Defense, 16
New York *Times*, 12, 29, 69; Colby's South American tour, 145, 152
New York *Tribune*, 145, 152
New York *World*, 12
Nicaragua, 122; electoral disorders, 138-139; Crowder mission, 139
North American Chamber of Commerce in Brazil, 147
Northern Securities Case, 8
Noyes, Pierrepont B., 37, 38

Obregón, Álvaro, 105, 107, reportedly friendly, 106; seeks settlement, 112-113; unfrank in negotiations, 115, 115n; awaits Harding administration, 116
Olney, Richard, 15
O Paiz, 148
Open Door policy (China): 1, 81, 82, 84, 88; and Consortium negotiations, 75-79
Ortiz, Fernando, 134

Page, Walter Hines, 15, 17
Palestine, 47, 48-50
Panama Canal, 15, 118
Pan Americanism; 117-119; and Colby's goodwill tour, 143, 145, 147, 148-149, 151
Pan American Union, 118
Paris Peace Conference, 5, 6, 40-41, 42, 48, 51, 56, 60, 121, 141; withdrawal of American Commissioners, 33-37; Ruhr, 38; Teschen, 42-46; cables and Yap, 89-92
Patriotic Union (Haiti), 120-121
Penzance-Halifax cable, 90
Pernambuco-Monrovia cable, 90
Pershing, General John J., 142, 143
Persia, 47, 47n

INDEX

Peru: Tacna-Arica dispute, 146n
Pesqueira, Roberto V., 109, 110, 111-112, 112-113, 115, 116
Phelan, James D., 94
Philadelphia *Inquirer*, 13n
Phillips, William, 18
Platt Amendment, 137
Poland, 20, 21, 60, 63; Teschen boundary dispute, 42-46; U.S. opposes expansionism, 56, 72-74, 74n; Russo-Polish War, 61, 61n, 64-65, 71-74; and non-recognition of Soviet Russia, 66-68; Danzig crisis, 72-73
Polk, Frank L., 12, 13, 14, 19, 42, 46, 47n, 56n, 64, 64n, 78n, 81n, 105n, 141; withdrawal of peace commissioners, 33-36; Ruhr occupation, 37-38; trade with Soviet Russia, 57; opposes changes in Cuban electoral laws, 134

Rappallo, Treaty of, 53
Raskob, John J., 153
Red Scare (Bolshevism), 59
Reed, James A., 18
Reparations, 37, 37n, 42n, 53-54, 70n
Rhineland High Commission, 37, 40n
Rio Grande do Sul (Cruiser), 146
Robins, Raymond, 62
Robinson, Joseph T., 26n
Roosevelt, Franklin D., 27, 29, 153; comments on Caribbean and Haiti, 121
Roosevelt, Theodore, 8, 13n
Root, Elihu, 15, 27, 29, 43n, 143, 147
Roumania, 36, 51, 53, 63
Rowe, Leo S., 118-119, 143
Royal Bank of Canada, 122-123
Ruhr. See Germany
Russell, John H., 123
Russell, William W., 128, 129
Russia, 20, 21; U.S. against dismemberment, 55-56; Soviets seek U.S. recognition, 57; trade, 58-60; Russo-Polish War, 61, 72-74; U.S. non-recognition of Soviet Russia, 61-71; Chinese Eastern Railway, 79-80, 85, 86, 87, 88-89; Japanese seizure of Northern Sakhalin, 86-87; Russian gold, 88n

Sakhalin, 86-87, 88
San Remo Conference, 40-41, 48, 50
Sèvres, Treaty of, 48

Shantung controversy, 94
Shidehara, Kijuro, 96, 97, 98-99, 100, 101
Shipping Board, 9, 10
Siberia. See Russia
Siebold, Louis, 145
Silva Pessôa, Epitacio da, 141, 142, 146
Smith, Alfred E., 153
Snowden, Admiral Thomas, 125, 127, 128, 129, 131-132, 132n
"Solemn referendum," 25-30
South America: Colby's goodwill tour, 141-152
Spa Conference, 42, 43, 44, 45
Spargo, John, 62, 64-65, 68, 74
Spartacists, 38, 40
Stabler, Herbert, 127
Standard Oil Company, 47, 48, 48n
Stephens, William D., 96, 98, 100
Stevens Technical Board, 88
Stimson, Frederic J., 144, 150
Submarine warfare, 3, 4, 15
Summerlin, George T., 106, 106n, 115, 115n
Sweden, 43n, 57, 74

Tacna-Arica dispute, 146n
Taft, William H., 9, 16, 17, 143n
Teschen boundary dispute, 42-46
Todd, Lawrence, 19n
Treaty of Riga, 74
Tumulty, Joseph, 10, 13, 18, 21
Turkey, 41, 48, 50, 92

Uchida, Viscount Yasuya, 95
Underwood, Oscar W., 24, 33
United States: discord with Allied Powers, 32, 33, 51, 53; recall of peace commission, 33-37; Ruhr occupation, 37-38; San Remo Conference, 40-41; Armenia, 41-42; Spa Conference, 42; Teschen boundary dispute, 42-46; commercial rivalry with Britain, 46-47; oil and mandates, 47-50; Fiume, 51-53; reduces role in postwar Europe, 53-55; policy toward Russia, 55-56; trade with Soviets, 55-60; Russo-Polish War, 60-61; non-recognition of Soviets, 62-71; negotiation of Consortium, 75-79; Anglo-American cooperation in Far East, 79-80; renewal of Anglo-Japanese Alliance,

INDEX

80-85; Chinese Eastern Railway, 85-86, 87-89; Northern Sakhalin, 86-87; cables and Yap, 89-92; alien land laws and Japanese immigration, 92-101; difficulties with Carranza, 101-105; negotiations with Obregón-Huerta regime, 105-116; retreat from Caribbean interventionism, 117-119; Haiti, 119-127; Dominican Republic, 127-133; avoidance of further intervention in Cuba, 133-138; disorders in Nicaragua, 138-139; Guatemala, 139-141; Honduras, 140n; Colby's goodwill tour of South America, 141-152

Uruguay, 142, 143, 144, 145, 148-149, 151

Versailles Treaty, 2, 18, 21-31, 32, 33, 34, 36, 37n, 38, 42, 52, 54, 72, 73

Walker, Harold (Mexican Petroleum Company), 105
Wallace, Hugh C., 34, 36, 37n, 38, 39, 42n, 56, 57, 71-72, 73; Teschen boundary dispute, 43-46; withdraws from Council of Ambassadors, 53-54
War Trade Board, 16
Washington Arms Conference, 92
Welles, Sumner, 118-119, 130, 130n, 143
Wellesley, Victor, 82
White, Henry, 33
Wilson, Edith Bolling, 5, 13, 20, 21, 33, 34, 35n, 36
Wilson, Woodrow, 1, 14, 15, 17, 62, 64n, 76n, 108, 126, 148; postwar bitterness, 2, 32; and Bryan, 2-4, 20n; and Lansing, 4-6, 20n; and Colby, 6, 7, 10n; appoints Colby Secretary of State, 10-14; Colby's earlier criticism, 15-16; House War Mission, 17; appointment of Norman Davis, 19; close relations with Colby, 20-21, 154; Senate and the Treaty fight, 21-31, 24n; League Assembly call, 25n; on Hoover, 22n; and a third nomination, 25-27; withdrawal of peace commissioners, 33-37; Ruhr occupation, 37-40; Armenia, 40-41; Spa Conference, 42; suspicions of Allies, 42, 46, 51, 53-55; Teschen dispute, 42-46; on Root, 43n; commercial rivalry with England, 46-47; oil and mandates, 47-50; Fiume, 51-53; Roumania and Bulgaria, 51, 53; trade with Soviets, 58-60; Russo-Polish War, 61n; and non-recognition of Soviets, 65-66, 68; Danzig, 72-73; writes Lloyd George, 74n; Consortium, 76, 77, 79; Chinese Eastern Railway, 80; renewal of Anglo-Japanese Alliance, 81; northern Sakhalin, 86-87, cables and Yap, 89-90, 91, 92; revision of Gentlemen's Agreement, 98; Lansing warns on Mexico, 104-105; Obregón-Huerta regime, 106-107; Creel mission to Mexico, 109; Mexican negotiations, 111, 113; Pan-Americanism, 117-119; Haiti, 119, 125, 125n; Dominican Republic, 130-131, 132-133; Cuban disorders and opposes force, 135, 136-137; Honduras, 140n; wartime visits with Latin America, 141; Colby's goodwill tour, 143-144, 149; Tacna-Arica dispute, 146n; cabinet farewell to, 152; law partnership with Colby, 152-153; relations with Bryan, Lansing, and Colby, 154, 155-157
World Court League, 16
Wrangel, General Peter N., 70n

Yap, 89-92
Yugoslavia, 51-53

Zara, 53
Zayas, Alfredo, 134